Olympiad ACE

A Comprehensive Practice Book

for School Olympiads & Talent Search Exams

MATHS

Class 5

BLOOM

Olympiad ACE

A Comprehensive Practice Book

for School Olympiads & Talent Search Exams

MATHS

Class 5

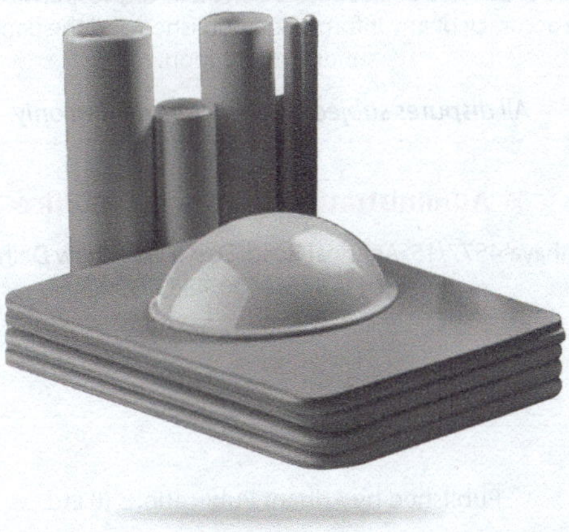

by

Mohit Soni

Olympiad ACE

BLOOM

Bloom Cap Edu Ventures Pvt. Ltd.

卐 **Administrative & Production Office**

'Ramchhaya' 4577/15, Agarwal Road, Darya Ganj, New Delhi -110002
Tele: 011- 47630600, 43518550

卐 **PRICE:** ₹125.00

Published by Arihant Publications (I) Ltd.

For further information about the books log on to
www.bloomcap.org

Follow us on

Preface

"Future belongs to those Who prepares for it today"

School Olympiads are National & International level competitions conducted by different Government, Non-Government & Educational Organisations with the purpose of making the children ready to face competitive exams. The challenging Questions asked in Olympiads motivate them to learn more & more and bring out the best result with improved academic performance. The Awards & Scholarship offered in Olympiads motivate children to aspire & strive for doing better and emerge out to be the best.

Maths Olympiads

Mathematics is an integral part of all competitive exams be it Aptitude or Commerce or Science. Maths Olympiads are meant to develop Mathematical aptitude in school students. They provide students with an opportunity to master their concepts and comprehend tricky questions effortlessly. Challenging Questions of Maths Olympiads encourage students to develop a logical approach to solve Mathematical Problems.

'Bloom Mathematics Olympiad Study Book Class 5' is a perfect resource to Study & Practice for Olympiad Exams and other National & State Level Talent Search Exams & Other Competitions.

Some Special Features of Bloom Maths Olympiad Study Books are;

- Chapterwise Exercises having different types of Objective Questions at par with the Olympiad Level.
- Detailed Explanation for each question.
- Olympiad Pattern Practice Sets at the end.

This book is prepared by Expert Panel with the utmost care, still if you have any suggestions regarding its improvement, then feel free to contact us at support@bloomcap.org. We will try to inculcate your suggestions in the further editions.

Contents

Chapter 01

Number System

1 Mark Questions

1. Fifty million fifty thousand fifty is same as

(a) 5050050 (b) 50500050
(c) 50500500 (d) 50050050

2. The area of Maharashtra is 8,725,651 sq km. Which system of numeration is used in the representation of the area of Maharashtra?

(a) International system
(b) Indian system
(c) Roman system
(d) None of the above

3. Ramia wrote four phone numbers in her diary but forgot to write the name of the respective persons. She could only remember that her friend's phone number had 8 in the thousand's place and 4 in the ten's place. Then, her friend's number is

(a) 469821 (b) 829824
(c) 578242 (d) 982431

4. While noting down the code number of a train from online railway site Maria wrote 14380502. How will she recite it to her brother correctly?

(a) One four three eighty thousand five hundred two
(b) One hundred forty three million eight thousand five hundred two
(c) One crore forty three lakh eighty thousand five hundred two
(d) Fourteen lakh thirty eight thousand five hundred two

5. In the number 5792456 the digit 7 stands for

(a) 7 hundred thousand
(b) 7 thousand
(c) 7 ten thousand
(d) 70 lakh

6. Difference between the place value and face value of 9 in the number 1297625 is

(a) 9 (b) 99991
(c) 89991 (d) 90001

7. What least number should be added to 3543467 such that place value of 1 in the resulting numeral becomes 100000000?

(a) 70000000 (b) 96456533
(c) 95634671 (d) 95465633

8. State 'T' for true and 'F' for false and mark the correct option.

I. Place value and face value are always equal for '0'.
II. Successor of a number is one less than the number.
III. Place value of a digit becomes 1000 times as it moves from ten's place to thousand's place.
IV. Commas are inserted in a number after each period.

	I	II	III	IV		I	II	III	IV
(a)	T	T	F	T	(b)	F	T	T	F
(c)	T	F	F	T	(d)	F	F	T	F

9. Choose the statement which is correct from the following given statements.

(a) 99999999 is the successor of 100000000

(b) The difference between the successor and predecessor of a number is 2

(c) '0' is the smallest one-digit number

(d) Face value and place value of a number are always same

10. The Jim Corbett National Park has an area of approximately 1217403 acre. This number in expanded form written as

(a) 12 lakh 17 thousand 4 hundred 3 ones

(b) 1 lakh 12 thousand 43 hundred

(c) 12 lakh 170 thousand 43 ones

(d) 120 thousand 40 tens 3 ones

11. While writing a number in expanded form a student missed a number as shown below :

$800000000 + 900000 + 10000 + 5000 + \_\_\_\_ + 8 = 800915018$

What is the number which he missed?

(a) 18 (b) 100 (c) 10 (d) 1080

12. Jack wrote the expanded form of number in words without using addition sign as follows. Nineteen lakh nineteen thousand nineteen hundred and nineteen.

The correct number he has written as

(a) 1920919 (b) 19191919

(c) 19192119 (d) None of these

13. In a certain state 5261989 students were enrolled in various schools. Of these 1965233 were primary school students and 2006756 were high school students, the rest attended middle school.

What is the number of students enrolled in middle school rounded off to nearest lakh?

(a) 2000000

(b) 1300000

(c) 1200000

(d) None of the above

14. Jivin made this table to show the number of visitors at 4 different beaches during one year.

Beach visitors

Beach	Number of visitors
Alligator point	12982
Port bella	12173
St. Joe's island	13704
Tucker's sound	12499

Which beach has number of visitors equal to 13000 when rounded off to nearest thousand?

(a) Tucker's sound (b) St. Joe's island

(c) Port bella (d) Alligator point

Directions (Q. Nos. 15 and 16) Use the table given below to answer the following questions.

Number of students participated in FBD's Olympiad

National FBD Science Olympiad	5748129
National FBD Maths Olympiad	6275492
National FBD English Olympiad	6275501

15. In which Olympiad the digit 5 is at one lakh place?

(a) National FBD Maths Olympiad

(b) National FBD Science Olympiad

(c) National FBD English Olympiad

(d) None of the above

16. Number of students who participated in National FBD English Olympiad to nearest ten thousand is

(a) 6200000 (b) 6280000

(c) 6000000 (d) 6285000

17. Ms. Hendrick's 5th grade class collected 2803 waste papers to recycle in one month and 3745 waste papers the next month. She estimated the total number of papers for both months by adding 3000 and 4000. Would her estimate be more or less than the actual answer?

(a) Less, because she rounded both numbers up

(b) More, because she rounded both numbers up

(c) Less, because she rounded both numbers down

(d) More, because she rounded both numbers down

18. Which of the following is the best estimate of the product 6842×59?

(a) 408000 (b) 340000
(c) 342000 (d) 403678

19. Using all the digits 7, 4, 0, 5 form the greatest possible 7-digit even number using all the digits where repetition of digit is allowed.

(a) 7540000 (b) 7775540
(c) 7755440 (d) 7777540

20. In the given abacus where should a ring (one) be added, so as to make the number lying between 24631 and 25212?

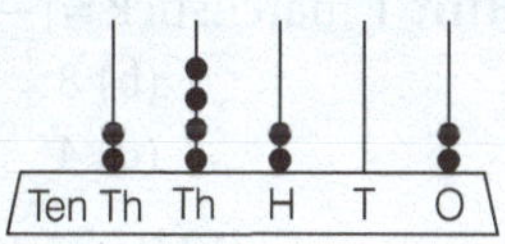

(a) One (b) Hundred
(c) Thousand (d) Ten thousand

21. A college students' union held a raffle to raise money for a musical concert. Amaira drew ticket number 392704, Samantha drew ticket number 396491, Barbara drew ticket number 392677 and Celia drew ticket number 396449. Whose ticket had the largest number?

(a) Celia (b) Samantha
(c) Amaira (d) Barbara

22. On comparing the numbers, the signs that will come in the given boxes are

I. 99999 ☐ 100000

II. 9909409 ☐ 9990409

III. 30100100 ☐ 30100099

	I	II	III		I	II	III
(a)	$>$	$<$	$=$	(b)	$<$	$<$	$>$
(c)	$=$	$>$	$>$	(d)	$>$	$>$	$<$

2 Marks Questions

23. Find the successor and predecessor of a number which is obtained by $673 \times 3719 - 473$ are $2502XY5$ and $P5\ Q2413$ then find the sum of $XY + PQ$.

(a) 5 (b) 3 (c) 4 (d) 7

24. The sum of place value of X and Y in the given numbers $54X973$ and $Y2635$ is 53000, then find the value of $3Y + 2X$.

(a) 17 (b) 19
(c) 53 (d) 21

25. Diwakar's user ID is a 6-digit number. Number 9 is in the ten thousands place. Number 0 is in the ones place. Number 6 is in Hundred thousands place. Number 8 is in the tens place. Number 4 is in the thousands place. Number 1 is in the hundreds place. What is Diwakar's user ID number?

(a) 964180 (b) 694180
(c) 691480 (d) 961480

26. Choose an answer that has a digit in the hundreds place that has a greater value than the digit in the thousands place but lesser value than the digit in the ones place.

(a) 102,266
(b) 638,941
(c) 580,343
(d) 574,567

27. Piyush is thinking of a 5-digit number. The unit's place digit is a even prime number. The ten's place digit is the predecessor of ten thousand's place digit. The hundred's place digit is the smallest odd prime number and the thousand's place digit is the smallest odd number. What could be the number Piyush is thinking of?

(a) 61352 (b) 51362
(c) 63512 (d) 63251

Chapter 02

Roman Numerals

1 Mark Questions

1. A student made a mistake while writing roman numeral for 495. He wrote CDCXV. How will you correct the mistake?

(a) C should be replaced by L.

(b) X should be replaced by C.

(c) Middle letter should be interchanged by the next letter.

(d) Middle letter should be interchanged by the last letter.

2. Where should C be placed in the Roman numeral CMXIX, so that it will represent 999?

(a) Right to the M

(b) Right to the I

(c) Left to the M

(d) Left to the I

3. The difference of roman numerals LXV – IX is

(a) LIV (b) LVI

(c) LV (d) LIII

4. CM represents a number. If place of the symbols is interchanged, the number will increased by

(a) 100 (b) 2000

(c) 1000 (d) 200

5. How many matchsticks are needed to make the roman numerals equivalent to 40? [**Hint** 1 matchstick = [—]]

(a) 5 (b) 8

(c) 12 (d) 4

6. The result of 'XLV ÷ III' in roman numeral is

(a) VX (b) XV

(c) X (d) XIV

7. If a bar is placed over L, then resultant value becomes ___ times of the value of D.

(a) 10 times

(b) 100 times

(c) 1000 times

(d) 10000 times

8. Using the digits 0, 2, 8 make the greatest 3-digit number without repeating the digits and write it in Roman numeral.

(a) DCCCXX (b) CMXX

(c) DCMX (d) CDCCXX

9. Which of these numbers has the least value?

(a) DCLX (b) CDCX

(c) CDXL (d) DCXL

2 Marks Questions

10. Write in ascending order of the following roman numbers.

XXI, XV, LIX, LXI, XXIX, XCIX

(a) XV<XXI<XXIX<LIX<LXI<XCIX
(b) XV>XXI<XIXX>LIX>LXI<XCIX
(c) VXI<XXI<XXV<LIV<XIL>XCXI
(d) None of the above

11. Find the roman numeral for 10638.

(a) $\overline{\text{XX}}$DCVIII (b) $\overline{\text{M}}$DCVIII
(c) $\overline{\text{V}}$DCXXXVIII (d) $\overline{\text{X}}$DCXXXVIII

12. K is a natural number which is equal to difference between 3 digit greatest number and 3 digit smallest number. What will be the roman numeral for K?

(a) CCMXCIX (b) DCCCLCIX
(c) DCCCXCIX (d) CMCXCIX

13. Some roman numerals are given in the box.

VIMCX

Which of the following is the number that can be written using all the given roman numerals?

(a) 1947 (b) 1548
(c) 1118 (d) 1753

14. Match the following.

A.	LXXXVIII	1.	39
B.	XCVIII	2.	69
C.	LXIX	3.	160
D.	CLX	4.	98
E.	XXXIX	5.	88

(a) A-(4), B-(5), C-(2), D-(3), E-(1)
(b) A-(5), B-(4), C-(2), D-(3), E-(1)
(c) A-(2), B-(1), C-(5), D-(3), E-(4)
(d) A-(1), B-(2), C-(5), D-(4), E-(3)

15. Suppose two roman numerals are DCCCVI and CCMVI, the correct relation is

(a) <
(b) >
(c) =
(d) None of the above

Chapter
03

Operations on Numbers

1 Mark Questions

1. Look at the below sum carefully and find in which one of the following column from right there is a mistake?

$$\begin{array}{r} 843671 \\ +\ 5329 \\ \hline 848000 \end{array}$$

(a) First (b) Second
(c) Third (d) Fourth

2. Find the number which is 2631 more than the number shown on the abacus.

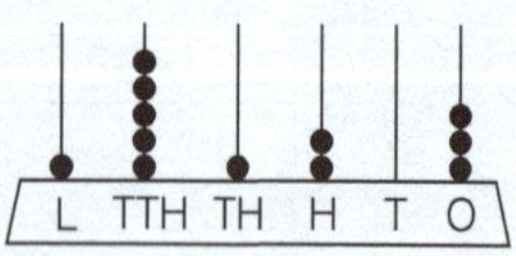

(a) 153834 (b) 151203
(c) 148572 (d) None of these

3. From the following numbers

277, 316, 479, 582

Choose the correct option that fill in the blanks to complete the following operation.

_____ − _____ = 305

(a) 479, 277 (b) 582, 277
(c) 582, 316 (d) 479, 316

4. If A, B and C are natural numbers and $A = 76240$ and $B = 3245$. If the sum of A and B is equal to the difference of C and B, then the possible value of C is

(a) 82730
(b) 72995
(c) 79485
(d) Cannot be determined

5. In a city, age of 34768 people is below 20, age of 57498 people is between 20 and 30 and age of remaining people is above 30. If the total population of the city is 100000, then the number of people who are above 30, is

(a) 92266 (b) 42502
(c) 65232 (d) 7734

6. Observe the number line given

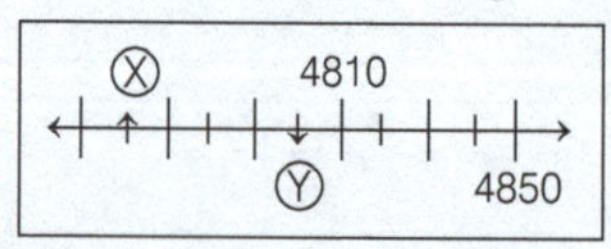

What is the difference of X and Y?

(a) 400 (b) 50
(c) 30 (d) 40

7. Make the six digit greatest and least number using the digits 8, 5, 9, 1, 2, 3 only once and find their difference.

(a) 862 (b) 861732
(c) 761740 (d) 861622

8. If △ + △ + □ = 225

△ − □ = 30

Then, the value of $\triangle$ is

(a) 90 (b) 80
(c) 95 (d) 85

9. Manisha bought four cupcakes that all cost the same amount. Which operation she must use to find the total cost of them, if cost of one cupcake is ₹ 10?

(a) Subtracting 10 from 4
(b) Adding 10 to 4
(c) Multiplying 10 by 4
(d) Dividing 10 by 4

10. If each letter represents a different number, then the number represented by ABCDE in the following operation is

$$\begin{array}{r} A\,B\,C\,D\,E \\ \times\ 4 \\ \hline 1\,2\,3\,4\,5\,6 \end{array}$$

	A	B	C	D	E
(a)	3	0	8	6	4
(b)	3	1	8	3	9
(c)	1	2	3	4	5
(d)	5	4	3	2	1

11. A car route is 9 km long. The car goes through the route 2 times each day. How many kilometres will the car drive in 5 days?

(a) 100 km (b) 50 km
(c) 10 km (d) 90 km

12. Maria asked her younger sister to pick a calculator which is not showing the correct calculation and give it for repair. Which of the calculator will her younger sister choose, if the calculator screen shows the given numbers?

(a) $45789 \times 1 = 45789$

(b) $4579 \times 0 = 0$

(c) $45789 \times 10 = 457890$

(d) $45789 - 0 = 45789$

13. A football team sold 215 youth tickets for ₹4 each and 467 adult tickets for ₹9 each. Which expression can be used to find how much more money the football team made on adult tickets than on youth tickets?

(a) $(215 \times 4) - (467 \times 9)$
(b) $(215 \times 9) - (467 \times 4)$
(c) $(467 \times 9) - (215 \times 4)$
(d) $(467 \times 4) - (215 \times 9)$

14. Complete the product of 17 and 56 using the box method given below and fill in the missing mumber.

17× 56

	10	7	
50	(i)	350	(iii)_____
6	60	(ii)	(iv)_____
			952

	(i)	(ii)	(iii)	(iv)
(a)	50	40	500	130
(b)	500	42	850	102
(c)	600	35	420	110
(d)	160	30	410	56

15. 2961 sweets were given to the children in an orphanage. Each child received 3 sweets. How many children were there?

(a) 8883 (b) 987 (c) 2964 (d) 2958

16. There are 15 rows of mango trees in a farm. Each row has 325 trees. Trees of 6 rows are cut down. The total number of remaining mango trees in the park is

(a) 2925 (b) 4875
(c) 1950 (d) None of these

17. State 'T' for true and 'F' for false and mark the correct option.

I. When any number is divisible by 1, the quotient is 1 only.
II. Number divisible by 10 must have zero as a unit digit.
III. $(4 \times 6) + (4 \times 10) = 4 \times (6 + 10)$

IV. The greatest number in the subtraction is called minuend.

	I	II	III	IV
(a)	F	T	T	T
(b)	T	T	T	F
(c)	F	F	F	T
(d)	T	F	F	T

18. Four students in Ms. Banerjee's class simplify the expression below :

$$7+21\div 3-8\times 2+9$$

The first step of each of the four students is shown in the table below :

Students	First step
Megha	7 + 21
Jasmin	3 − 8
Sanchi	21 ÷ 3
Kruti	2 + 9

Which student performs a first step that is correct?

(a) Megha (b) Jasmin
(c) Sanchi (d) Kruti

19. Which number will come in the start box to have a meaningful proceeding?

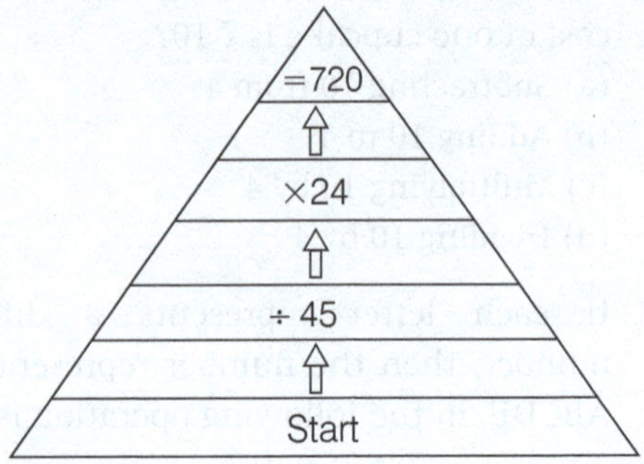

(a) 360 (b) 384
(c) 1350 (d) 1.50

2 Marks Questions

20. If $A+A+A+A+A+A+A+A+A+A+A=25465099$, find the value of $4A$?

(a) 2315009 (b) 9260036
(c) 9260360 (d) 2315090

Directions (Q. Nos. 21 and 22) The table below shows the number of food items collected by four classes for a donation camp. It also shows the number of days each class collects food items during the donation program.

Class	Packets of food items (per day)	Days collected
Class 1	728	25
Class 2	225	40
Class 3	374	20
Class 4	280	30

21. Which class collected the maximum number of food items?

(a) Class 1 (b) Class 2
(c) Class 3 (d) Class 4

22. If class 2 has to collect the same number of packets in 40 days as collected by class 1 in 25 days, then how many packets class 2 has to collect in one day?

(a) 728 (b) 210
(c) 455 (d) 242

23. If the product of 695 and $52AA72A$ is 3645083180, then find the value of $1015\times A$?

(a) 1015 (b) 4006
(c) 5075 (d) 4060

24. Find the value of $(A+B)-(C+D)$ by completing the given addition matrix.

+	5,345	7,200
4,520	A	B
9,100	C	D

(a) 9120 (b) −9160
(c) 9160 (d) −9120

Chapter 04

Factors and Multiples

1 Mark Questions

1. Which of the following shows the correct factorisation of 90?

(a) 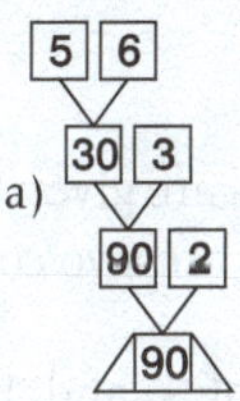

(b) 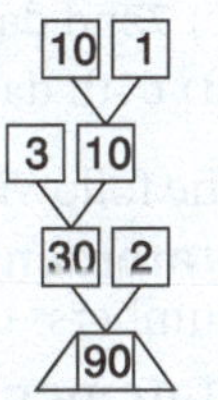

(c) 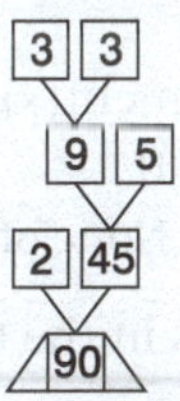

(d) 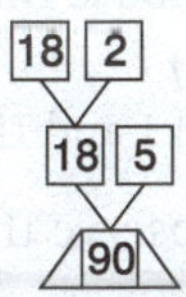

2. The following figure shows the factor tree of 150. On the basis of factor tree, fill the missing numbers and choose the correct option.

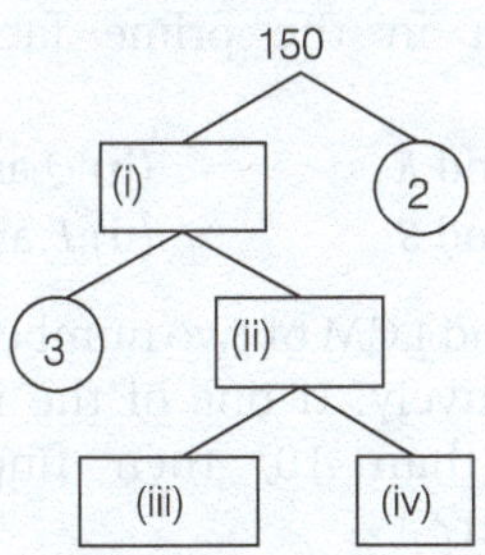

	(i)	(ii)	(iii)	(iv)
(a)	25	15	3	5
(b)	75	25	5	5
(c)	50	10	2	3
(d)	148	72	16	4

3.

Jamaica
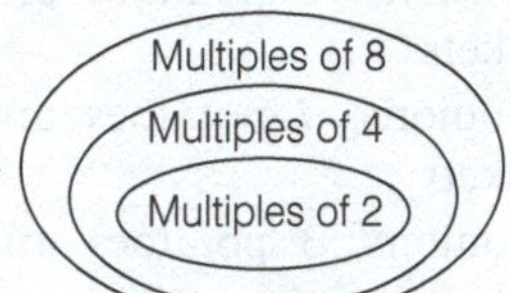

Kathy
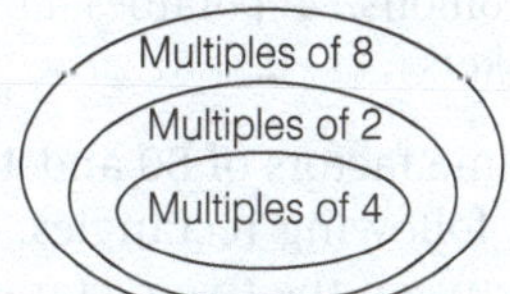

Jimmy
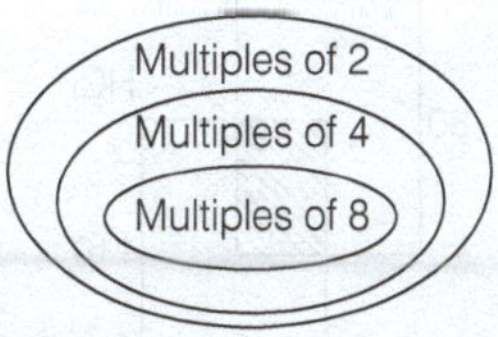

Who drew the correct picture?

(a) Jamaica
(b) Kathy
(c) Jimmy
(d) None of the above

4. The missing number in triangle II on the basis of the rule followed in triangle I is

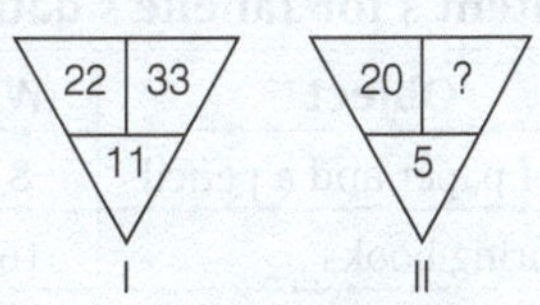

(a) 10 (b) 15
(c) 40 (d) 30

Directions (Q. Nos. 5-6) A vegetable vendor wants to pack 56 onions, 32 potatoes and 64 tomatoes in baskets containing an equal number of vegetables of same type.

5. What is the maximum number of vegetables of same type in each basket can he keep?

(a) 10 (b) 8
(c) 7 (d) 12

6. How many number of baskets of each type of vegetable will be made?

(a) 7 onions, 4 potatoes and 8 tomatoes baskets
(b) 5 onions, 7 potatoes and 6 tomatoes baskets
(c) 8 onions, 3 potatoes and 6 tomatoes baskets
(d) 6 onions, 4 potatoes and 7 tomatoes baskets

7. The prime factors of 80 and 110 are shown by the following rectangles. The common area between the two rectangles will have

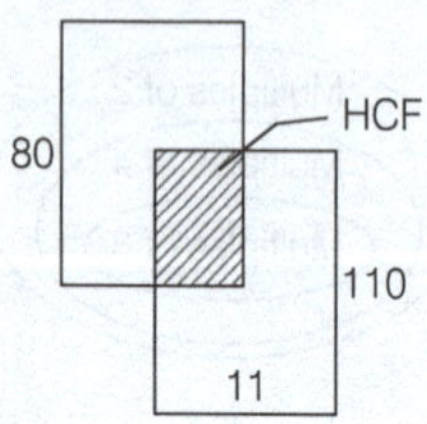

(a) 2×5 (b) 5×11
(c) $2 \times 5 \times 11$ (d) 11×2

8. Janelle is sending different contents on her daughter's hostel address. Following is the content list :

Content's for Janelle's daughter

Object	Weight
Pad of paper and a pencil	8 units
Colouring books	16 units
Dictionary	4 units
Toy	14 units

If these contents are to be packed separately in packets of same weight, then what would be the maximum weight of the packets having same weight?

(a) 4 units (b) 8 units
(c) 7 units (d) 2 units

9. Sonia intended to complete her three books in such a way that she reads Book *A* on every 4th day, Book *B* on every 5th day and Book *C* on every 6th day. On which day will she read all the three books together?

(a) 50th day
(b) 60th day
(c) 72nd day
(d) 64th day

10. The following statements are given below

Statement I If *X* and *Y* are two coprime numbers, their HCF is 1.

Statement II If HCF of *X* and *Y* is *X*, then *Y* is divisible by *X*.

Choose the correct statement(s).

(a) I (b) II
(c) I and II (d) None of these

11. Observe the twin primes in the table.

(3, 5)	(5, 7)	(11, 13)	(17, 19)
P	*Q*	*R*	*S*

Which of the given twin primes are present in the prime factorisation of 4845?

(a) *P* and *R* (b) *Q* and *R*
(c) *Q* and *S* (d) *P* and *S*

12. HCF and LCM of two number are 4 and 48 respectively. If one of the numbers is 2 more than 10, then find the other number?

(a) 19
(b) 20
(c) 18
(d) 16

2 Marks Questions

13. In a Mathematics paper, score of three girls are as follow

Annie Lowest multiple of 10

Jass Fourth multiple of 3

Krish Highest factor of 15

Which of the following is correct about the score of the girls?

(a) Annie < Jass < Krish

(b) Jass < Annie < Krish

(c) Krish < Annie < Jass

(d) None of the above

14. Margret joined three activities i.e. singing, dancing and drawing.

I. She went for singing class once in every 3 days.

II. She went for dancing class once in every 4 days.

III. She went for drawing class once in every 6 days.

The calendar below shows that Margret did all the activities on Monday 5th.

NOVEMBER

S	M	T	W	T	F	S
				1	2	3
4	5	6	7	8	9	10
11	12	13	14	15	16	17
18	19	20	21	22	23	24
25	26	27	28	29	30	

On which day will Margret again do all three activities on the same day?

(a) 12th, Monday (b) 17th, Saturday

(c) 21st, Wednesday (d) 30th, Friday

15. In an amusement park, a fountain erects water, in different colours at different intervals of time. The water of colour red comes out at every 40 minutes, of colour blue comes out at every 50 minutes and of colour yellow comes out at every hour. If the water of all the colours came out together at 8 am. At what time will they come out together again?

(a) 3 pm (b) 12 noon

(c) 6 pm (d) 8 pm

16. In the following figure, both figures are follow similar relation. On the basis of their relations, the value of x is

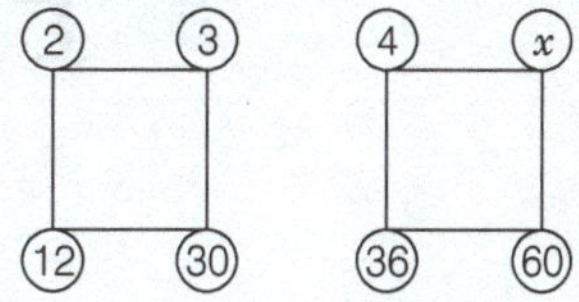

(a) 5 (b) 4

(c) 6 (d) 24

17. Study the following.

M is the least common multiple of 18, 24 and 40.

N is the highest common factor of 60, 180 and 360.

Which digit in the number $5M + 15N$ is on the thousands place?

(a) 0 (b) 1 (c) 2 (d) 3

18. Rosy and Luke are playing a game called "Guess my numbers."

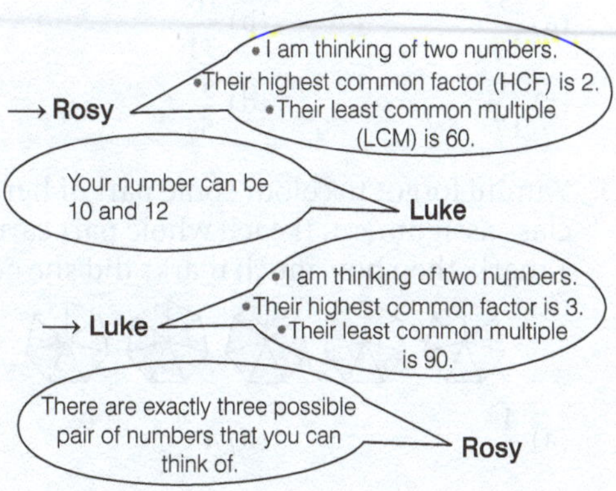

Who gave the correct answer to the other question?

(a) Rosy (b) Luke

(c) Both (a) and (b) (d) None of these

Chapter 05

Fractions

1 Mark Questions

1. What part of fraction vowels have of consonants in English alphabets?

(a) $\frac{5}{26}$ (b) $\frac{21}{26}$

(c) $\frac{5}{21}$ (d) $\frac{21}{5}$

2. While writing the answers to the questions given to Zeba in homework, she made a mistake in writing one of the answer in simplest form. Pick the answer she wrote incorrectly?

(a) $\frac{3}{15}$ (b) $\frac{16}{31}$

(c) $\frac{9}{17}$ (d) $\frac{4}{5}$

3. Yamini forgot to colour some part of her art class assignment. If each whole part carries 1 mark, then how much marks did she get?

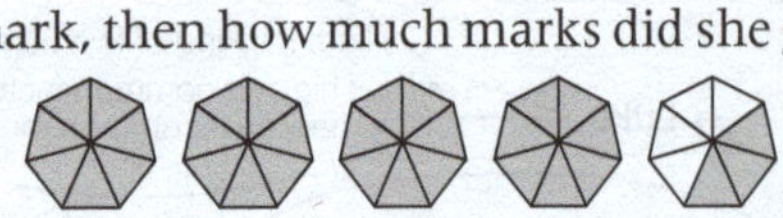

(a) $\frac{4}{5}$ (b) $4\frac{4}{7}$

(c) $4\frac{3}{7}$ (d) $\frac{1}{5}$

4. Pamela drew a picture using different shapes. What part of the picture has stars in it?

(a) $\frac{1}{2}$ (b) $\frac{1}{3}$

(c) $\frac{1}{4}$ (d) $\frac{2}{3}$

5. How many minimum unshaded rectangles should be added to make the figure $\frac{2}{3}$ part shaded?

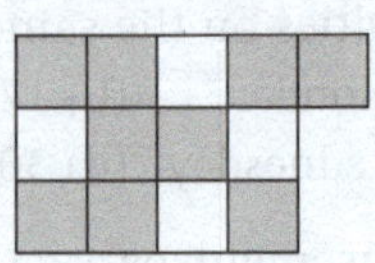

(a) 2 (b) 1

(c) 3 (d) 4

6. Which point on the number line represents $1\frac{9}{10}$?

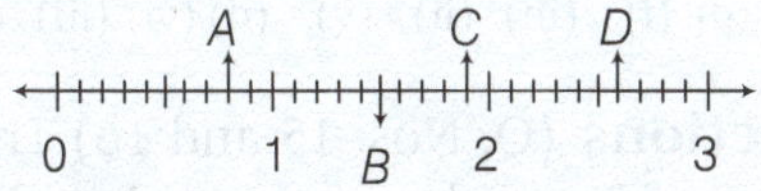

(a) A (b) B
(c) C (d) D

7. Mario made some holes in a triangle as shown in the picture. Determine the fraction to represent the part of triangles having odd number of holes.

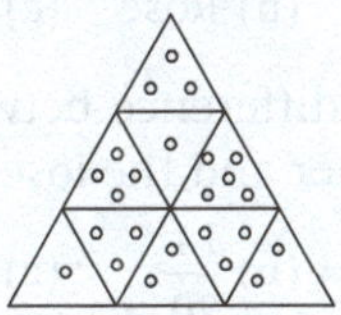

(a) $\frac{1}{3}$ (b) $\frac{4}{9}$
(c) $\frac{5}{9}$ (d) $\frac{2}{3}$

8.

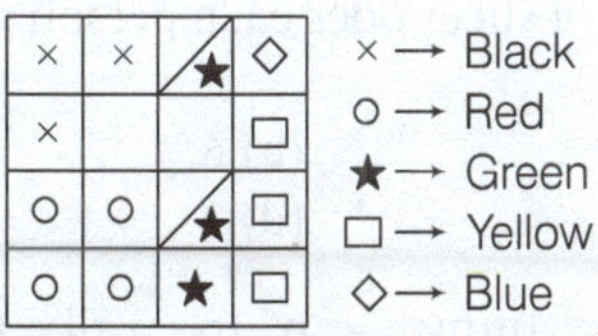

Above figure shows the different colours filled in the squares.

Match the following columns.

Column A	Column B
I. Red	(i) $\frac{1}{8}$
II. Green	(ii) $\frac{1}{16}$
III. Blue	(iii) $\frac{1}{4}$

	I	II	III		I	II	III
(a)	(i)	(ii)	(iii)	(b)	(iii)	(i)	(ii)
(c)	(i)	(iii)	(ii)	(d)	(ii)	(i)	(iii)

9. Which of the situations given below can be represented by the fraction $\frac{8}{24}$?

(a) 8 friends share 24 pies equally. How much pie does each person get?

(b) Grimmy sleeps 8 hours each day (24 hours). What part of each day does Grimmy sleep?

(c) Mark uses 2 dozen bananas to make banana shakes for his 8 children. How many bananas are in each shake?

(d) 24 toys are distributed into 8 groups. How many toys are received by each group?

10. Greg ate the following part of the cake and left the remaining for his friends. What part of cake did Greg eat?

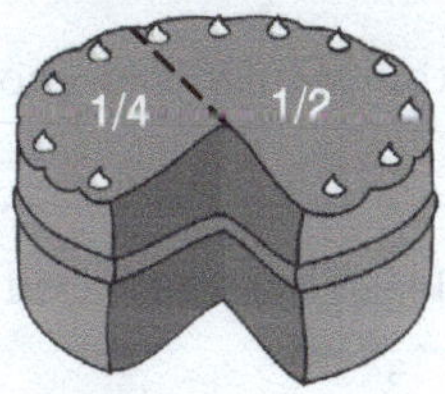

(a) $\frac{1}{2}$ (b) $\frac{3}{4}$ (c) $\frac{1}{4}$ (d) $\frac{2}{6}$

11. Eric had 12 weeks of summer vacation. He practiced guitar and learned 6 new songs. How many songs did Eric learn each week?

(a) 2 songs (b) 10 songs
(c) 5 songs (d) $\frac{1}{2}$ of a song

12. Tom talked on the telephone to three friends. He talked to Hary for $\frac{1}{6}$ h, to Geet for $\frac{5}{3}$ h and to Ryan for $\frac{1}{4}$ h. How much time did Tom spend on the telephone?

(a) $3\frac{1}{6}$ h (b) $2\frac{1}{12}$ h
(c) $4\frac{1}{6}$ h (d) $3\frac{1}{12}$ h

13. State 'T' for true and 'F' for false and mark the correct option.

I. $\frac{2}{5}$ is equivalent to $2 \times \frac{1}{5}$.

II. Fifteen $\frac{1}{10}$'s make $2\frac{2}{5}$.

III. 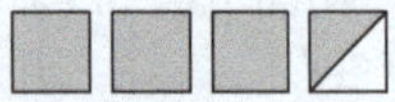 represent $3\frac{1}{2}$,

if  = 1.

IV. $\frac{2}{3}, \frac{4}{6}, \frac{18}{27}$ are all improper fractions.

	I	II	III	IV
(a)	F	F	T	T
(b)	F	T	F	T
(c)	T	F	T	F
(d)	T	T	F	F

14. Fill in the blanks and choose the correct option.

(i) proper	(ii) like	(iii) $\frac{5}{4}$
(iv) $-\frac{3}{7}$	(v) 0	(vi) improper
(vii) unlike		(viii) $\frac{-4}{5}$

I. $\frac{16}{13}$ is a/an .... fraction.

II. The multiplicative inverse of $\frac{4}{5}$ is ....

III. The fractions having different denominators are called .... fractions.

IV. The additive inverse of $\frac{3}{7}$ is

Codes

	I	II	III	IV		I	II	III	IV
(a)	(vi)	(viii)	(ii)	(iv)	(b)	(i)	(viii)	(vii)	(v)
(c)	(i)	(iii)	(ii)	(v)	(d)	(vi)	(iii)	(vii)	(iv)

Directions (Q. Nos. 15 and 16) The score of players in a video game is given below

Ken	Shim	Rose	Jack	Den
$\frac{75}{100}$	$\frac{46}{50}$	$\frac{54}{60}$	$\frac{72}{100}$	$\frac{89}{100}$

15. Who scored the highest?

(a) Ken (b) Rose (c) Shim (d) Den

16. What is difference between the score of the winner and the loser?

(a) $\frac{1}{5}$ (b) $\frac{14}{20}$ (c) $\frac{13}{100}$ (d) $\frac{15}{40}$

17. The local pizza place cuts their pizzas into sixths, so that each slice is $\frac{1}{6}$ of the pizza. If 8 people share the four pizzas, then the number of slices does each person get will be

(a) 4 (b) 6
(c) 8 (d) 3

18. It takes Jinny $\frac{5}{6}$ h to walk to the playground and $\frac{1}{4}$ h to walk from the playground to school. How much time does it takes Jinny to walk to the playground and then to school?

(a) $\frac{12}{19}$ h (b) $1\frac{1}{13}$ h
(c) $1\frac{1}{12}$ h (d) $\frac{12}{13}$ h

2 Marks Questions

19. A distance from 0 to 1 is divided into fourteen equal parts. Then, what fraction of B's distance is covered by A?

(a) $\frac{3}{4}$ (b) $\frac{3}{14}$

(c) $\frac{5}{14}$ (d) $\frac{15}{14}$

20. What fraction of the given figure is shaded?

(a) 7/16 (b) 4/16

(c) 5/16 (d) 6/16

21. If Fig. I represents 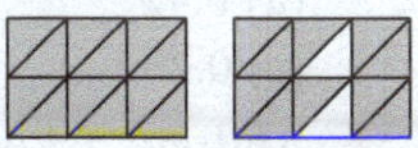

and Fig. II represents 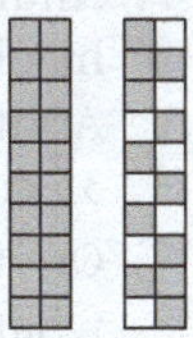 .

Then, which of the following is true for the fraction of shaded parts in figures I and II?

(a) I > II (b) II > I

(c) I = II (d) I ≤ II

22. Find the missing number

$$3\frac{3}{20}\times 2\frac{1}{3}+2\frac{1}{2}-\left(5\frac{2}{7}\div\frac{1}{7}\right)=?\times 270\frac{3}{2}$$

(a) $\frac{41}{10}$ (b) $-\frac{1}{20}$ (c) $-\frac{1}{10}$ (d) $\frac{1}{10}$

23. Read the given statements carefully and state 'T' for true and 'F for false.

(i) The shaded fraction of the given figure is $\frac{1}{2}$.

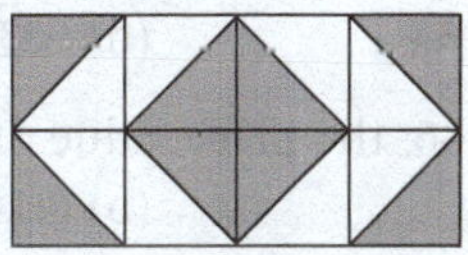

(ii) If a bag contains 3 red, 5 green and 9 yellow balls, then the fraction of green balls in the bag is $\frac{5}{17}$.

(iii) There are 21 sixth is $3\frac{1}{3}$.

	(i)	(ii)	(iii)		(i)	(ii)	(iii)
(a)	F	T	F	(b)	T	F	F
(c)	T	F	T	(d)	T	T	F

Chapter
06

Decimals

1 Mark questions

1. 90 ones 3 tenths and 4 hundredths is written as

(a) 90.34 (b) 90.034
(c) 900.34 (d) 903.4

2. In 12.146, the place value of the digit 4 is

(a) 4 (b) 0.14
(c) 0.4 (d) 0.04

3. Write the decimal $700 + 40 + \dfrac{5}{10000}$ is standard form.

(a) 740.005 (b) 704.0005
(c) 740.0005 (d) 740.5

4. Convert the decimal 98.25 into fraction.

(a) $\dfrac{9825}{1000}$ (b) $\dfrac{393}{4}$
(c) $\dfrac{98}{25}$ (d) $\dfrac{143}{51}$

5. What is the sum of the numbers represented by the letters A and B marked on the number line given below?

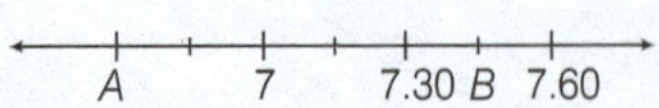

(a) 14.05 (b) 16.71
(c) 14.15 (d) 16.19

6. The shaded parts of this picture show what decimal number?

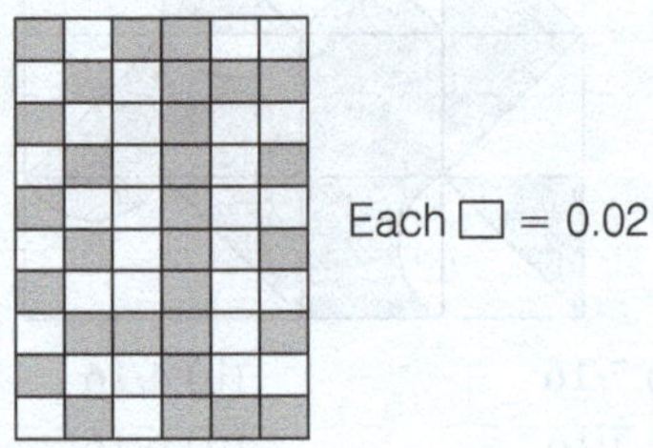

(a) 0.42 (b) 0.58
(c) 0.28 (d) 0.29

7. Andrew asked her sister to measure his height. Her sister after measuring Andrew's height said, "You have to grow 35 cm more to reach 2.5 m height."
On the basis of his sister's comment, what is the present height of Andrew?

(a) 0.6 m
(b) 1.25 m
(c) 2.15 m
(d) 2.85 m

8. If $A = 31.36$ and $B = 45.63$. Then, the value of $(2A - B)$ is equal to

(a) 17.09 (b) 30.70
(c) 18.79 (d) 23.63

Directions (Q. Nos. 9 and 10) Four identical paint pots of 2 L are being used by the painter and the following quantity of paint is left behind.

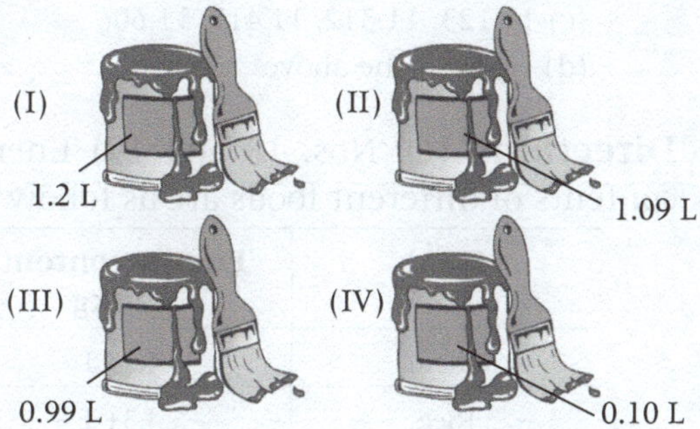

9. What is the total quantity of paint left?

(a) 3.38 L (b) 3.9 L
(c) 4.2 L (d) 13.99L

10. The difference between the maximum and minimum quantity of paint used is

(a) 0.99 L (b) 1.1 L
(c) 1.09 L (d) 1.2 L

11. I am a decimal number. My decimal part is 3 less than $\left[\frac{1}{4} \text{ of } 32\right]$ and my whole part is 2 more than $\left[\frac{2}{5} \text{ of } 20\right]$. What am I?

(a) 10.8 (b) 10.05
(c) 10.5 (d) 8.8

12. Fill in the blanks and choose the correct option.

(i) 0.90	(ii) 0.24
(iii) 9.01	(iv) 9.1
(v) 9.07	(vi) 9.0
(vii) 0.06	(viii) 0.625

I. The fraction $\frac{6}{25}$ is equal to decimal number ______ .

II. 15.8 – 6.73 is equal to ______ .

III. 9.07 rounded off to nearest tenth is ______ .

IV. 9.037 rounded off to nearest tenth is ______ .

	I	II	III	IV
(a)	(viii)	(v)	(vii)	(iv)
(b)	(viii)	(iii)	(v)	(i)
(c)	(ii)	(vi)	(iii)	(iv)
(d)	(ii)	(v)	(iv)	(vi)

13. In the following magical stairs, a relation given between the numbers on stair, find the missing number and choose the correct option.

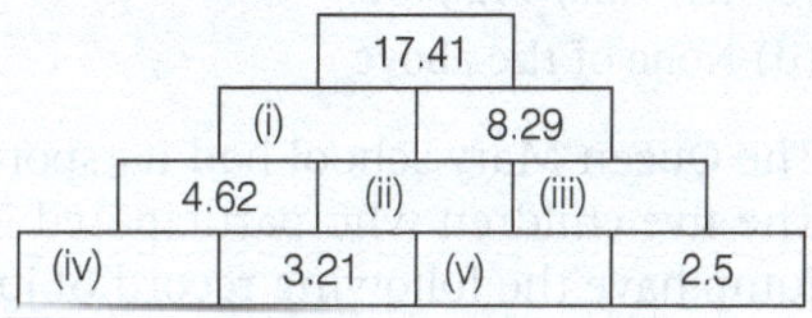

	(i)	(ii)	(iii)	(iv)	(v)
(a)	8.79	6.5	2.79	2.41	3.19
(b)	9.21	5.5	3.29	0.41	2.29
(c)	9.12	4.5	3.79	1.41	1.29

(d) None of the above

14. State 'T' for true and 'F' for false and choose the correct option.

I. 15.73 rounded to nearest tenth is equal to 15.7.

II. 6 hundredth is written as 0.60.

III. The digit 5 in 24.56 stands for 5 hundredths.

IV. 0.023 lies between 0.2 and 0.3.

	I	II	III	IV
(a)	T	F	F	F
(b)	F	T	T	F
(c)	T	F	F	T
(d)	F	T	T	T

15. A bill collection machine round off the numbers correct to two decimal places and then give the result. What will be the output of that machine?

Input	Output
4.123	–
7.299	–
14.756	–
0.014	–

(a) 4.12, 7.30, 14.76, 0.01
(b) 4.13, 7.29, 14.76, 0.02
(c) 4.3, 7.20, 14.8, 0.1
(d) None of the above

16. The Queen Mary school had its sports day. The five children who participated in long jump have the following record of jumps :

Alex	4.50 m
Amena	4.06 m
Ornald	3.99 m
Florence	3.09 m
Giba	4.28 m

Who won the long jump competition?
(a) Alex (b) Ornald
(c) Giba (d) Florence

17. Which of the following is in correct ascending order?
(a) 5.231, 5.219, 5.143, 5.424
(b) 7.128, 6.723, 3.825, 8.113
(c) 11.123, 11.312, 11.415, 11.606
(d) None of the above

Directions (Q. Nos. 18 and 19) Energy contents of different foods are as follow :

Food	Energy content per kg
Wheat	4.25 J
Rice	4.31 J
Potatoes (Cooked)	4.72 J
Milk	4.09 J

18. Arrange the food items in ascending order of the energy provided by them.
(a) Wheat < Rice < Potatoes < Milk
(b) Milk < Wheat < Rice < Potatoes
(c) Potatoes < Rice < Wheat < Milk
(d) None of the above

19. The total energy provided by all the food items is
(a) 14.37 J
(b) 15.74 J
(c) 17.37 J
(d) None of the above

2 Marks Questions

20. $A = 917.35, B = 434.17$ and $C = 1201.234$

Then which of the following expressions will hold the value 2986.924?

(a) $2A + B + C$ (b) $A + 2B + C$

(c) $A + 2B + 2C$ (d) $3A + 4B + C$

Directions (Q. Nos. 21 and 22) Tyran and his two younger sisters, of age 9 yr and 10 yr respectively, are going to see a movie that starts at quarter to 6.

Cinema 1	Cinema 2
Invasion from Mars 12:30, 2:15, 4:00, 5:45, 7:30, 9:15	The Museum Mystery 12:45, 2:30, 4:15, 6:00, 7:45, 9:30
Adults ₹ 6.00 Children (under 12) ₹ 3.75	

21. Tyran is paying for the three tickets. He is 9 years older than his youngest sister. How much will he spend for tickets?

(a) ₹ 18.25 (b) ₹ 16.75

(c) ₹ 13.5 (d) ₹ 13.75

22. Tyran and his sisters plan on spending a total of ₹ 2.75 for snacks whereas their parents plan on spending a total of ₹ 4.35.

What will be the total cost of tickets and snacks for the entire family?

(a) ₹ 32.6 (b) ₹ 28.1

(c) ₹ 30.75 (d) None of these

Directions (Q. Nos. 23 and 24) Divine parked his bike from 10 am to 6 : 50 pm on Monday and Sunday. The charges of parking are given below :

Time	Charges (weekdays)	Charges (Saturday/ Sunday Public holidays)
6 am to 11 am	₹ 1.50 per hour	₹ 1.20 per hour
11 am to 5 pm	₹ 2.20 per hour	₹ 1.80 per hour
5 pm onwards	₹ 0.50 every half hour	₹ 2.20 per half hour

23. How much did Divine have to pay in total for the parking charges on Monday?

(a) ₹ 16.7 (b) ₹ 10.5

(c) ₹ 28.4 (d) ₹ 4.2

24. How much cheaper did he pay for the parking charges on Sunday than on Monday?

(a) ₹ 0.1 (b) ₹ 4.1

(c) ₹ 4.2 (d) None of these

Chapter 07

Measurement

1 Mark Questions

1. Ella walked once around the given track. How far did Ella walk?

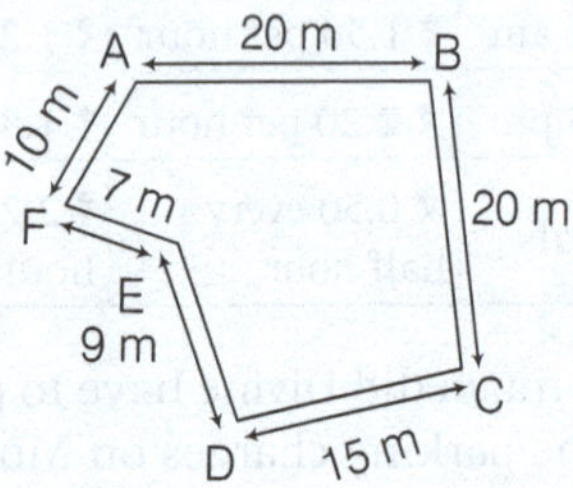

(a) 810 cm (b) 8100 cm
(c) 81 cm (d) None of these

2. Angelina planted rose flowers on the boundary of her house. She has placed the plants 8 cm apart from each other.

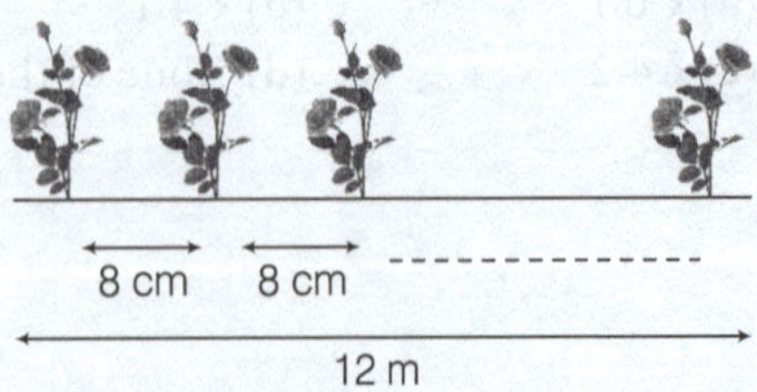

If the length of the boundary and the sequence of plants is as given, then how many such plants can be planted?

(a) 150 (b) 151 (c) 160 (d) 164

3. Jessy was 1 m 25 cm tall last year. This year, he is 12 cm taller. How much taller is Jessy than Teresa now, if Teresa is 1 m 8 cm tall?

(a) 10 cm (b) 25 cm
(c) 29 cm (d) 10 cm

4. In Banaras and Kolkata, women wear sarees of length 8.28 m long. If a yard is equal to 0.92 m. Then, how much do they measure their sarees in yards?

(a) 8 yards (b) 7 yards
(c) 9 yards (d) 6 yards

5. Michelle bought a shirt for her brother but some how its length was short. Her brother asked her to get it exchanged and buy a shirt of length 4 inch greater than this. If the length of the shirt is 58.5 cm, then what is the length of the shirt Michelle's brother want?

(given, 1 inch = 2.5 cm)

(a) 95.5 cm (b) 48.9 cm
(c) 68.5 cm (d) 58.9 cm

6. If object C weighs 4 kg 800 g, then find the mass of object B.

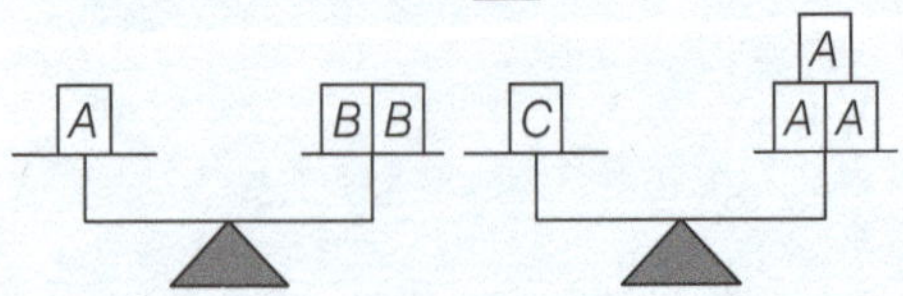

(a) 500 g (b) 600 g
(c) 800 g (d) 1000 g

7. A tailor had a piece of cloth. He cut 4 smaller pieces of cloth each $\frac{3}{5}$ m from it. If he had left with $4\frac{3}{5}$ m of cloth, then the total length of the cloth is

(a) 5 m (b) 7 m
(c) 4 m (d) 6 m

8. Study the following diagram. If the weight of 1 square = 5 circles and 1 triangle = 4 circles, then the number of circles required on the other side of the scale to balance the scale is

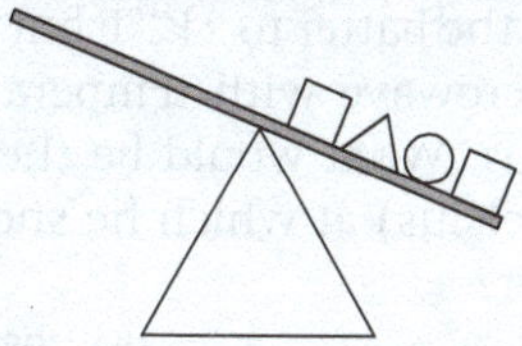

(a) 12 (b) 15
(c) 21 (d) 3

9. Aleena had two pieces of gold as 6 kg 755 g and 5 kg 550 g, respectively. She wanted to get a gold biscuit weighing 15 kg. How much more gold does she need?

(a) 1 kg 795 g (b) 2 kg 795 g
(c) 1 kg 695 g (d) 2 kg 675 g

10. State 'T' for true and 'F' for false and choose the correct option.

I. Mixing 3.6 kg of orange candy with 0.75 kg of yellow candy and packing them in 5 boxes of equal weight will make each box of weight 0.87 kg.

II. If Vandy having height $1\frac{3}{8}$ m is $\frac{1}{4}$ m shorter than Andy, then Andy is $1\frac{1}{8}$ m tall.

III. If 13338 L of oil is poured in 9 cans equally, then weight of each can is 14.82 L.

IV. Length of a book is measured in litres.

	I	II	III	IV
(a)	F	T	F	F
(b)	T	F	F	F
(c)	F	F	F	F
(d)	T	T	F	T

11. Michael wanted to find the volume of a spherical ball but could not remember the formula.

He used a measuring glass and pour some water in it. After dropping one ball in the glass, the water is raised to level as shown below

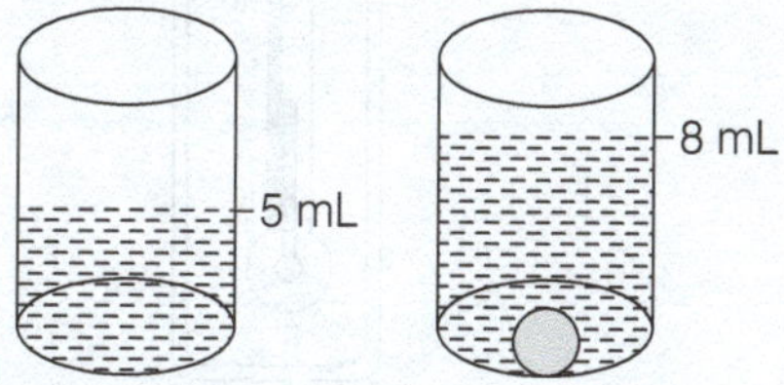

Similarly four more balls of equal size are droped in the glass.

If 1 mL = 1 cm^3, then what is the total volume (in cm^3) of ball?

(a) 12 (b) 15
(c) 18 (d) 13

12. If ten buckets of same volume are used to fill the given bath tub, then the volume of one such bucket is

(given, 1 m^3 = 1000 L)

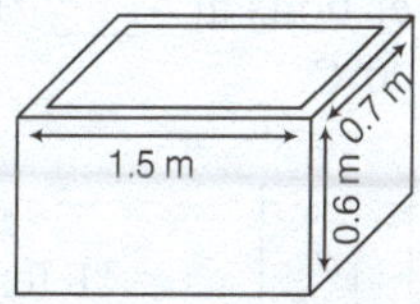

(a) 63 L (b) 6.3 L
(c) 630 L (d) None of these

13. Martini have a big bucket. He needs to put 1 L of water in it for his science experiment but he only have 150 mL and 25 mL containers. How many times does he need to use each of the container to fill in the bucket?

(a) 150 mL → 4 times and 25 mL → 6 times
(b) 150 mL → 8 times and 25 mL → 3 times
(c) 150 mL → 6 times and 25 mL → 4 times
(d) None of the above

14. If $°C = (°F - 32) \times \frac{5}{9}$, then what is the temperature shown by the given thermometer in celsius?

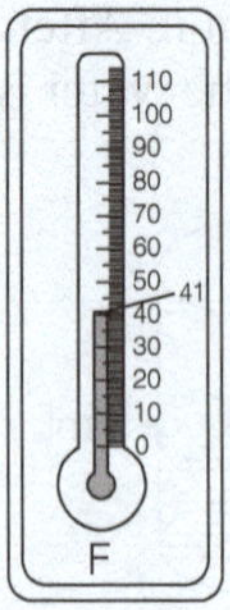

(a) 10°C (b) 5°C
(c) 23°C (d) 18°C

15. Braiden have to bake a cake for his sister's birthday party. He noted down the recipe from internet and started preparing for it. The recipe instructed to bake the batter to 212°F but Braiden have a microwave with temperature given in celsius. What would be the temperature (in celsius) at which he should bake the batter?

(a) 0°C (b) 70°C
(c) 100°C (d) 212°C

2 Marks Questions

16. Fill in the blanks and choose the correct option.

(i) 100	(ii) 32	(iii) 212	(iv) 95
(v) 35	(vi) 50	(vii) 10	

I. Water freezes at 0° C which is same as _____ °F.

II. Water boils at _____ °F which is same as 100°C.

III. 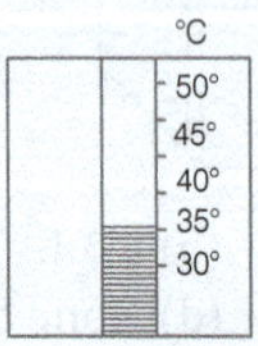

_____ °F temperature is shown by the thermometer.

IV. The difference of 35°C and 25°C in fahrenheit is _____ ° F.

	I	II	III	IV
(a)	(ii)	(iii)	(iv)	(vi)
(b)	(iii)	(i)	(v)	(vi)
(c)	(iii)	(ii)	(vi)	(v)

(d) None of the above

17. Temperature of two hot vessels containing water is shown below

What is the difference (in °F) of the temperature of the vessels?

$$\left[\text{if } °F = °C \times \frac{9}{5} + 32\right]$$

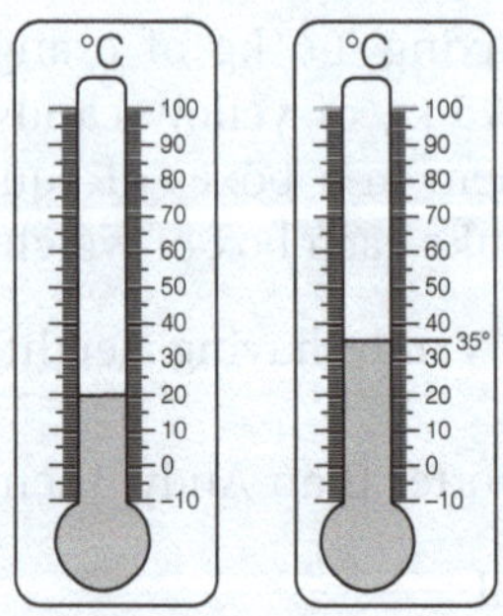

(a) 60° F
(b) 20° F
(c) 59° F
(d) 39° F

18. Read the statements carefully and select the correct option.

Statement-1 Value of weight of 12 such balls is 9th multiple of 30.

Statement-2 Weight of 8 such balls is 67 g more than weight of 5 such balls.

(a) Both Statement-1 and Statement-2 are true.

(b) Statement-1 is true but Statement-2 is false.

(c) Statement-1 is false but Statement-2 is true.

(d) Both Statement-1 and Statement-2 are false.

19. Mr. Gredwick and his workers had to pack 140 cubical shape boxes to be delivered to a shop. They made three boxes having square box of sides 30 ft, 20 ft and 10 ft respectively and having equal height of 12 ft each. If all the boxes got completely packed without leaving any space, then what would be the volume (in cubic ft) of each of the small box?

(a) 120 (b) 140

(c) 160 (d) 180

20. Kavya started studying at time shown below. After 2 h 15 min, she stopped and took some rest. She then again studied for another 1 h 45 min and then stopped at the time shown. How long was her rest period?

(a) 50 min

(b) 1 h

(c) 1 h 05 min

(d) 55 min

Chapter

08

Shapes and Angles

1 Mark Questions

1. A hunter throws an arrow to kill a deer but it lands on the ground as shown in the picture. What type of angle does it make with the ground ?

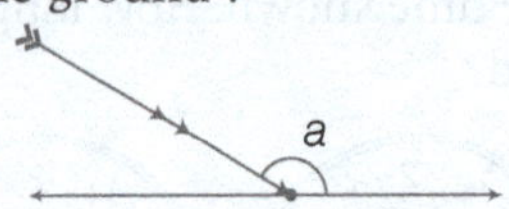

(a) Obtuse (b) Right
(c) Straight (d) Acute

2. Pick the odd one out from the following sign boards on the basis of the angle formed.

(a) (b) (c) (d)

3. Choose the correct matched option from the following.

	Column A		Column B
I.	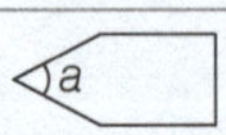	(i)	Reflex angle
II.	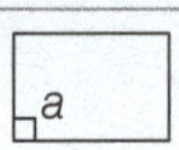	(ii)	Acute angle
III.	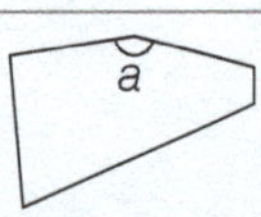	(iii)	Right angle
IV.	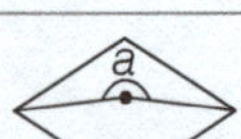	(iv)	Obtuse angle

	I	II	III	IV
(a)	(ii)	(iv)	(i)	(iii)
(b)	(i)	(ii)	(iii)	(iv)
(c)	(iv)	(i)	(ii)	(iii)
(d)	(ii)	(iii)	(iv)	(i)

4. A road map of an area is given below. It has 4 roads drawn. Which of the angles marked in the map is an obtuse angle?

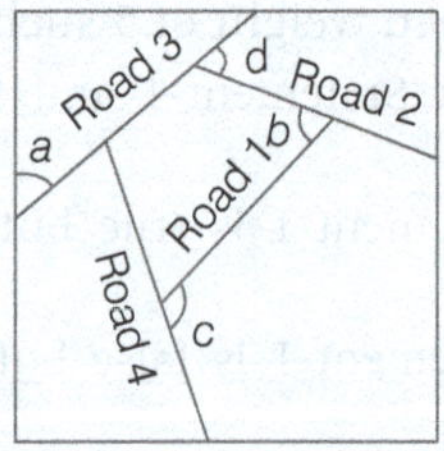

(a) Angle a (b) Angle b
(c) Angle c (d) Angle d

5. When the legs of a table are stretched to open, the angles formed from the top of the table as shown in the figure. Identify which of the angles are obtuse and which are acute

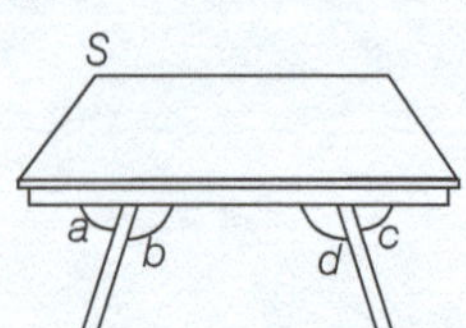

(a) $\angle a$, $\angle b$, are acute $\angle c$, $\angle d$ obtuse
(b) $\angle a$, $\angle c$ acute $\angle c$, $\angle d$ obtuse
(c) $\angle b$, $\angle d$ acute $\angle a$, $\angle c$ obtuse
(d) $\angle a$, $\angle d$ acute $\angle b$, $\angle c$ obtuse

6. 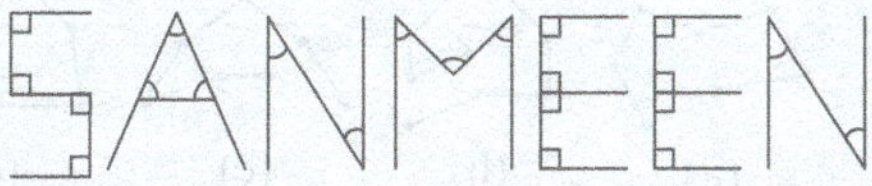

Mr. Raman wrote a name on the blackboard and asked the students to count the number of acute angles formed. Four students stood up and had different answers as follows

Neil There are nine acute angles.

Shimer There are twelve acute angles.

Jany There are ten acute angles.

Trini There are fifteen acute angles.

Who is correct in counting the number of acute angles?

(a) Neil (b) Shimer
(c) Jany (d) Trini

7. A sign of swastik is given in the adjoining figure. How many right angles are there in the given figure?

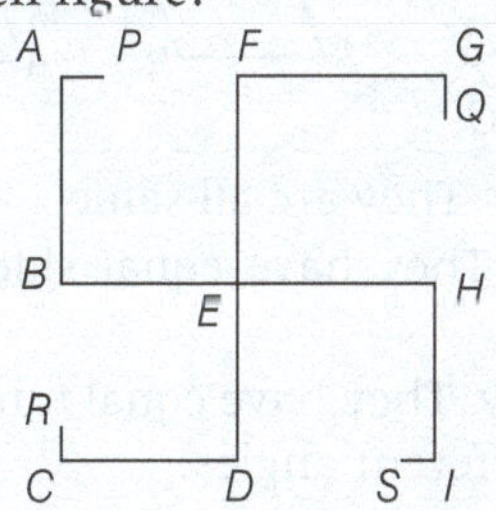

(a) 8 (b) 10
(c) 12 (d) 6

8. 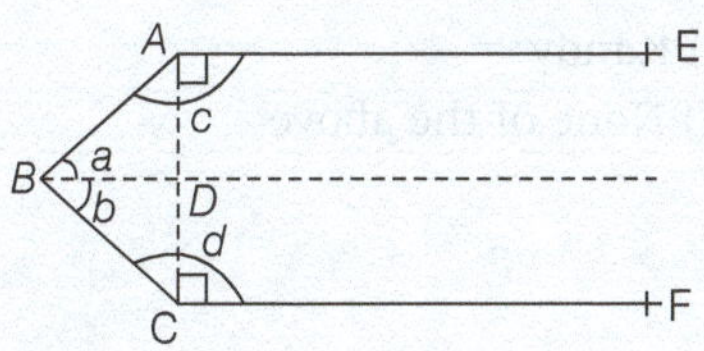

The figure given above show different angles mode by joining the lines then which of the following statement is true regarding angles

I. Only angles *a* and *b* are acute angles

II. There is no right angle in the given figure.

III. ∠c and ∠d are obtuse angles.

(a) I, II (b) II, III
(c) I, III (d) Only II

9. Fill in the blanks and choose the correct option.

(i) 90°	(ii) 180°
(iii) 270°	(iv) 45°
(v) 42°	(vi) 41°

I. Half of a right angle is ______ .

II. Turning $\frac{3}{4}$ anti-clockwise means turning by an angle of measure ______ anti-clockwise.

III. Folding a circular sheet into halves two times will form a ______ angle.

IV. If ∠ABC is a right angle, then ∠DBE is equal to ______ .

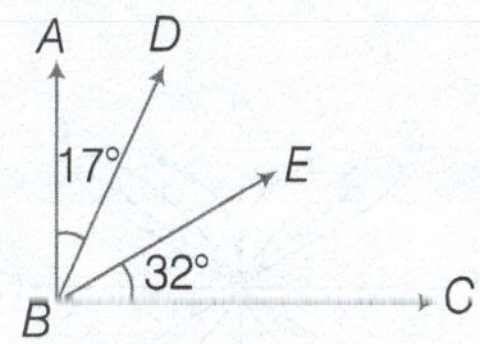

	I	II	III	IV		I	II	III	IV
(a)	(i)	(ii)	(iii)	(iv)	(b)	(iv)	(iii)	(vi)	(v)
(c)	(iii)	(i)	(iv)	(v)	(d)	(iv)	(iii)	(i)	(vi)

10. State 'T' for true and 'F' for false and choose the correct option.

I. Different shapes can be formed using same number of sides.

II. Alphabet 'L' forms a right angle.

III. A rectangle and a square have equal angles.

IV. Turning $\frac{1}{4}$ clockwise or anti-clockwise means to turn at an angle 60°.

	I	II	III	IV		I	II	III	IV
(a)	T	T	F	F	(b)	F	F	T	T
(c)	F	F	F	F	(d)	T	T	T	F

11. The hour hand of the clock given below is turned 90° clockwise and then 180° anti-clockwise. Which angle will be formed by the minutes and hour hands of the clock after rotation?

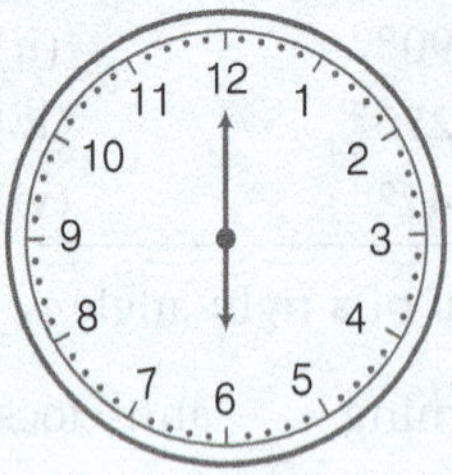

(a) 45° (b) 90°
(c) 180° (d) 60°

12. A butterfly structure is shown in the given figure. If the vertical line AB and horizontal line CD, then identify what angle each half wing (*OP*, *OQ*, *OR* and *OS*) of butterfly will make with these horizontal and vertical lines

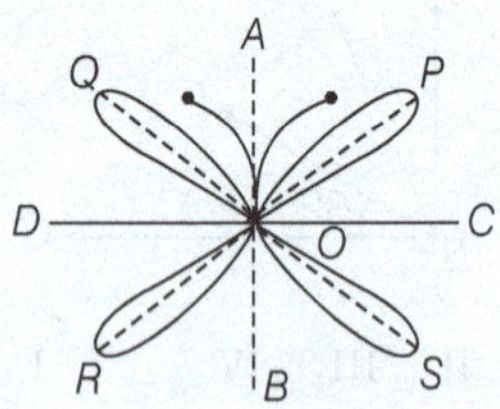

(a) 30° (b) 60°
(c) 90° (d) 45°

13. Richard uses matchsticks and forms some shapes with them. Which of the shapes formed by him is different from others?

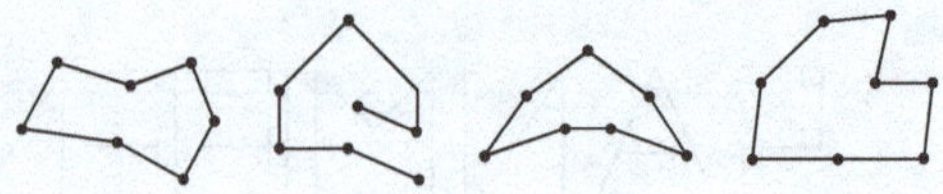

(a) (b) (c) (d)

14. Compare the following shapes on the basis of the number of right angles in each one and choose the correct option.

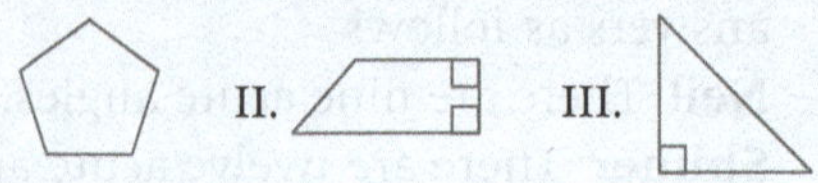

I. II. III.

(a) I > II > III
(b) I < II < III
(c) II > III > I
(d) III > II > I

15. Shane drew some shapes and asked his friends to find the difference between them.

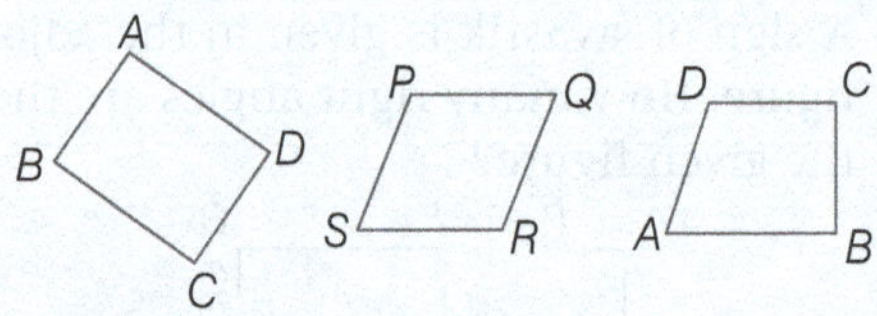

Jenny They are all same.
Kim They have equal sides and equal angles.
Kandy They have equal number of sides but different angles.
Who said the correct statement?
(a) Jenny
(b) Kim
(c) Kandy
(d) None of the above

2 Marks Questions

16. Study the given figure and answer the following questions.

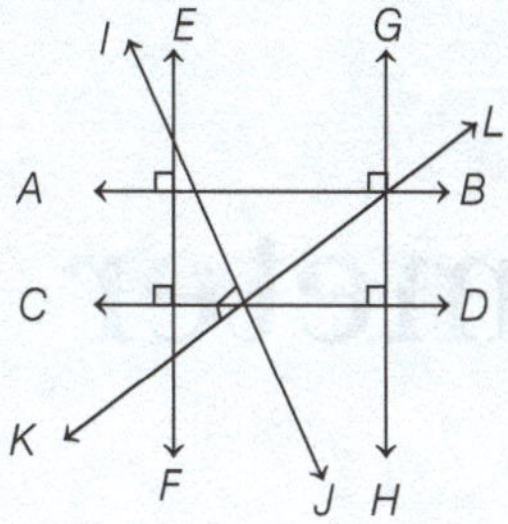

(i) Number of pair of parallel lines is /are ......

(ii) Number of pair of perpendicular lines are

	(i)	(ii)		(i)	(ii)
(a)	2	3	(b)	2	4
(c)	1	3	(d)	2	5

17. Observe the figure given,

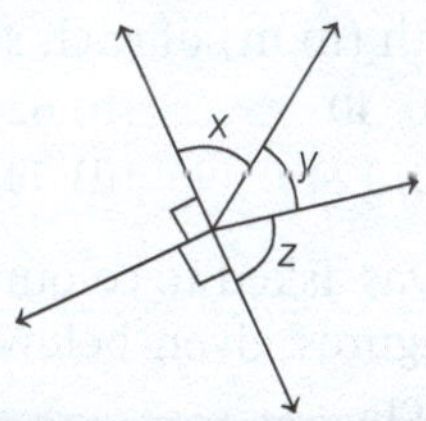

What is the measure of $x+y+z$?

(a) 90° (b) 180°

(c) 270° (d) 360°

18. Max went to the playground to get rides. He liked playground slides the more, so he went on sliding on two different slides having different slopes, based on the angle made with the ground.

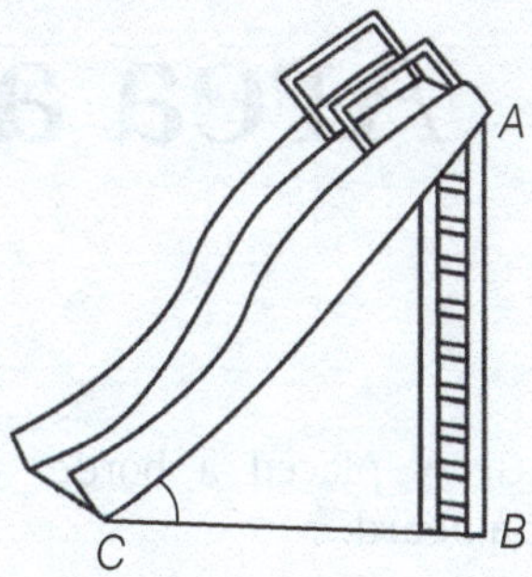

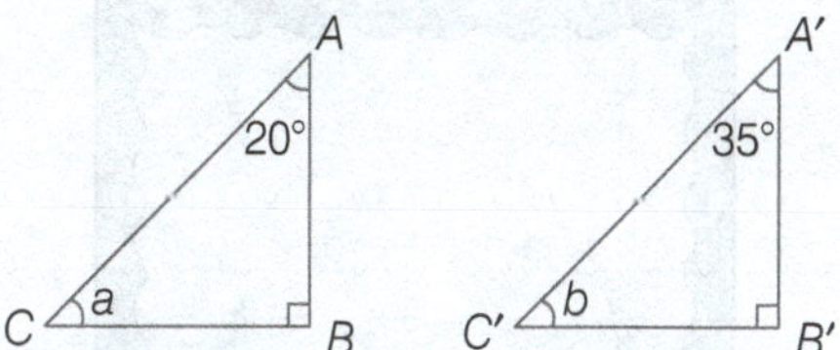

Playground slide I   Playground slide II

The angles made by each slide with the ground are

(a) 70°, 45°

(b) 80°, 65°

(c) 70°, 55°

(d) 80°, 45°

Chapter 09

Area and Perimeter

1 Mark Questions

1. Mrs. Gerry placed a border around the bulletin board.

The length of the border is an example of

(a) area

(b) volume

(c) perimeter

(d) circumference

2. Trini has a project to decorate the boundary of a shape given below with a ribbon. How much ribbon will be used to decorate the boundary?

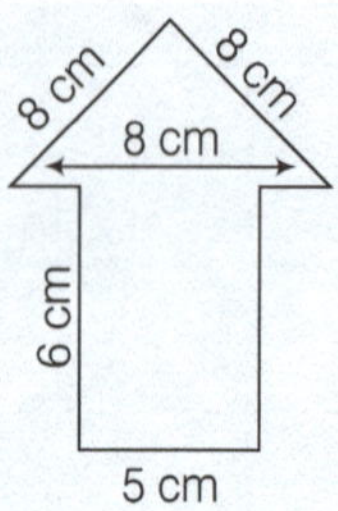

(a) 40 cm (b) 41 cm

(c) 36 cm (d) 32 cm

3. Find the length of third side of a triangle whose perimeter is 280 m and length of two sides are 75 m and 125 m.

(a) 60 cm (b) 80 cm

(c) 120 cm (d) 200 cm

4. The ratio of the sides of a triangle is 2 : 3 : 4 and its perimeter is 279 m, find the length (in m) of each side.

(a) 20, 30, 40 (b) 62, 90, 120

(c) 62, 93, 124 (d) 54, 78, 104

5. Sanjay was asked to colour the boundary of the figures given below with a black sketch pen.

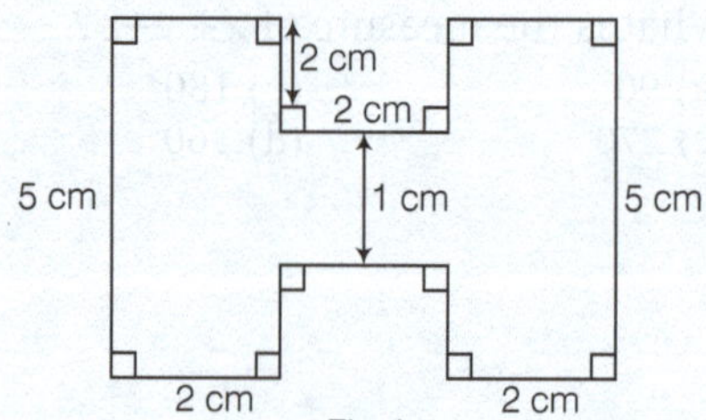

Fig. I

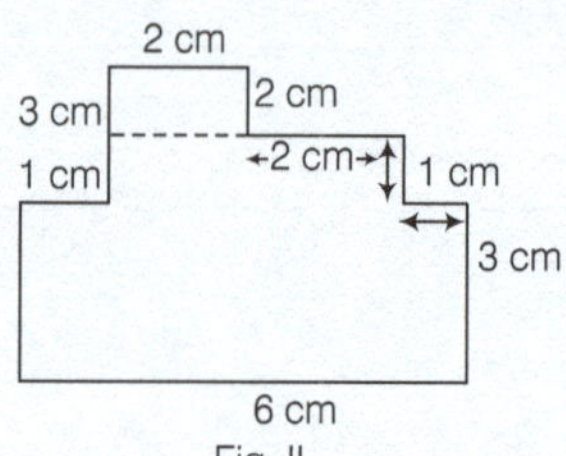

Fig. II

In which figure he needs to colour the boundary more?

(a) I
(b) II
(c) Both I and II
(d) Cannot be determined

6. Mrs. Bishop wanted to make a frame for her family picture. She marked the picture to help her figure out the perimeter of the picture. What is the perimeter of Mrs. Bishop picture?

(a) 54 cm (b) 30 cm
(c) 28 cm (d) 60 cm

7. Jolly and Ted built pens for their dogs as given in the picture.

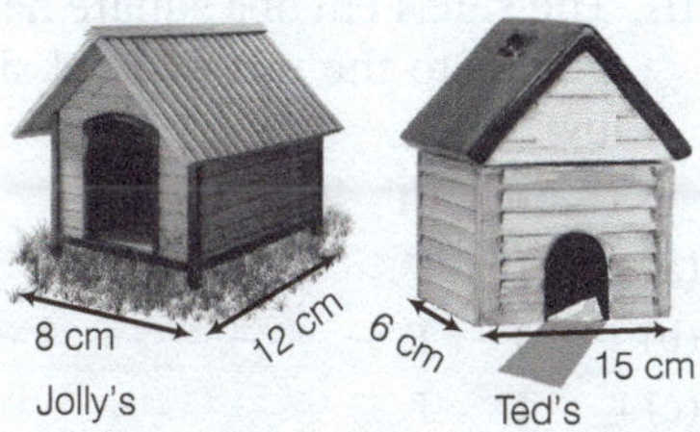

Who among them used more fencing to build the bottom of the pen?

(a) Ted
(b) Jolly
(c) Both will use same
(d) Cannot be determined

8. Jessica while making her doll house, arranged some cubes to build stairs for it as shown below

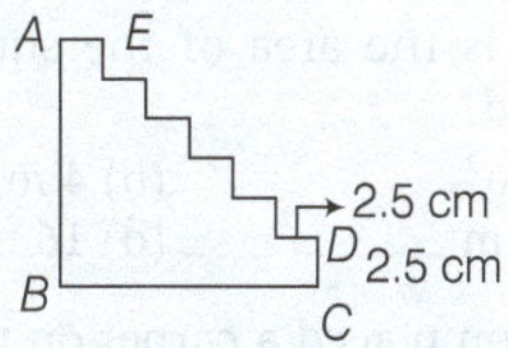

What is the perimeter of the corner *ABCDE* of the stairs, if the dimensions are as given in figure?

(a) 45 cm
(b) 60 cm
(c) 30 cm
(d) Cannot be determined

9. A picture given below shows the area of the land being used for farming in a city. Using this picture, find the area of the land used for farming shown by the shaded portion.

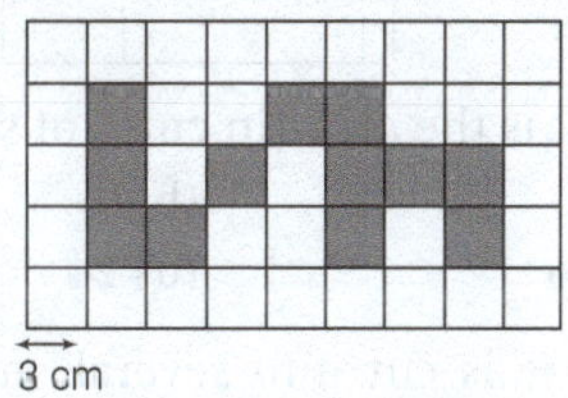

(a) 108 cm^2 (b) 72 cm^2
(c) 12 cm^2 (d) 9 cm^2

10. Krish made a windmill for his Science project. He made the blades of the windmill by using wooden sticks of size 6 m. These sticks overlapped each other and formed the square *ABCD*.

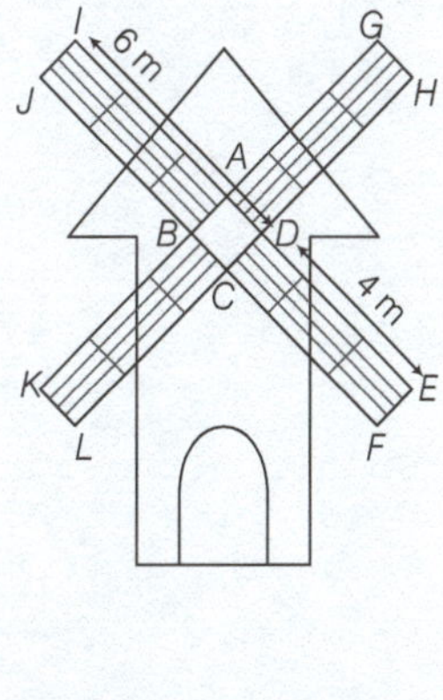

What is the area of the square *ABCD*, so formed?

(a) 2 m^2 (b) 4 m^2
(c) 24 m^2 (d) 16 m^2

11. Addison placed a carpet on the floor of his drawing room but found it to be of the exact size. He wanted to leave a border of 2 ft on each side. If the carpet measures 12 ft by 10 ft. Then, the area of the border is

(a) 48 sq ft (b) 72 sq ft
(c) 120 sq ft (d) 100 sq ft

12. Maria had a length of wire 40 cm long. She bent the wire to make the following shape, where *X* and *Y* are squares.

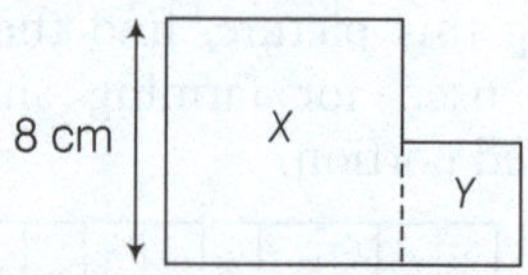

What is the area (in cm^2) of square *Y*?

(a) 6 (b) 9
(c) 16 (d) 24

13. A wire is cut into several smaller pieces. Each of the smaller pieces are bent into two squares. The perimeter of square I and area of square II are as follow :

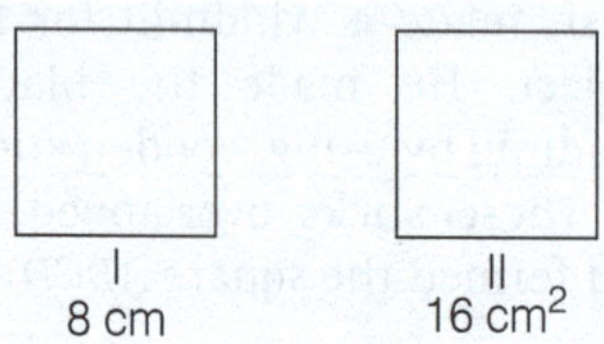

What is the length of the wire?

(a) 20 cm (b) 12 cm
(c) 24 cm (d) 18 cm

14. Find the area of the rectangle whose perimeter and length are 36 cm and 12 cm respectively.

(a) 72 cm^2 (b) 48 cm^2
(c) 24 cm^2 (d) 90 cm^2

15. Which of the following are the dimensions of a rectangle with a perimeter of 26 inch and an area of 42 sq inch?

(a) Length-1 inch, width-26 inch
(b) Length-2 inch, width-13 inch
(c) Length-2 inch, width-21 inch
(d) Length-6 inch, width-7 inch

16. State 'T' for true and 'F' for false and choose the correct option.

I. The perimeter of a rectangle formed by joining two squares of side 4 cm is 24 cm.

II. If the sides of rectangle are doubled, then its area will also be doubled.

III. The side 4 cm of a square having area equals to the rectangle of sides 8 cm by 2 cm

	I	II	III
(a)	T	F	T
(b)	T	T	F
(c)	T	F	F
(d)	F	T	T

2 Marks Questions

Directions (Q. Nos. 17 and 18) A king decided to honour his two soldiers for their bravery in the field of war against their enemies.

He asked one of them to choose any shape of land having a boundary of measure 100 m.

17. What type of land the soldier must choose in order to have the maximum area of land?

(a) Rectangle

(b) Square

(c) $\frac{1}{2}$ rectangle + $\frac{1}{2}$ square

(d) None of the above

18. The king asked the other soldier to choose a land having area equal to 400 m^2 and he will give him as much length of silver wire as the boundary of that land. Which type of land will he choose from below?

(a) 20 m × 20 m (b) 40 m × 10 m

(c) 4000 m × 0.1 m (d) None of these

19. A classroom of dimensions 18 ft by 22 ft had 28 benches each of size 4 ft and 2.5 ft, an almirah of dimensions 5 ft by 4 ft and a table of size 3 ft by 5 ft. How much space is left in the class room now?

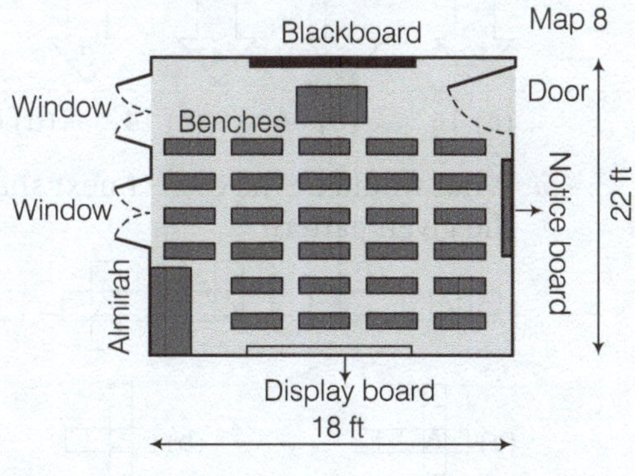

(a) 81 sq ft

(b) 72 sq ft

(c) None of the above

(d) Cannot be determined

Directions (Q. Nos. 20 and 21) A map of school is given in the picture. Answer the following questions on the basis of it considering that each class has same area and dimensions.

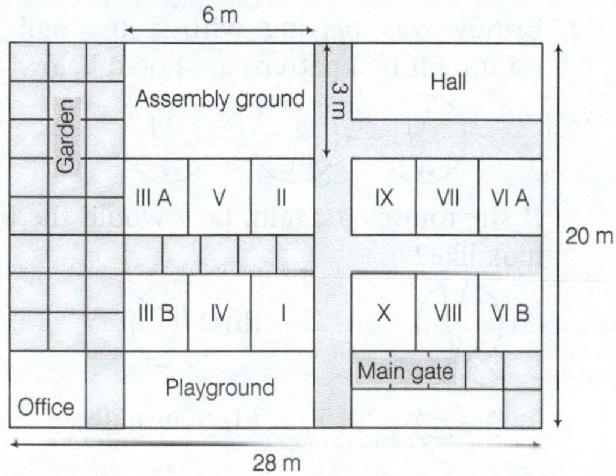

20. If each class has same area and length of each of the class is 4 m. Then, what is the area covered by classes given in the picture?

(a) 12 m^2

(b) 8 m^2

(c) 96 m^2

(d) 144 m^2

21. If area of hall is $\frac{2}{3}$ times the area of assembly ground, then what is the perimeter of the hall?

(a) 16 m^2 (b) 4 m^2

(c) 22 m^2 (d) 26 m^2

Chapter 10

Pattern and Symmetry

1 Mark Questions

1. Brindy was playing with a toy ball by rotating it in a pattern as shown below

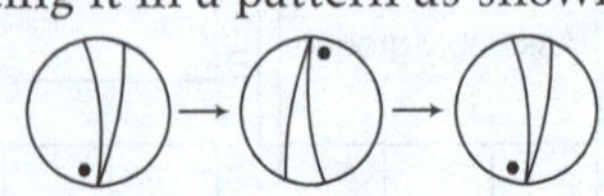

If she rotates it again, how would the ball look like?

(a) 

(b) 

(c) 

(d) None of these

2. In an art class, a teacher taught students how to make symmetrical pattern by blotting ink and then folding the paper. One of the student tried the activity and formed a shape, half of which is given alongside.

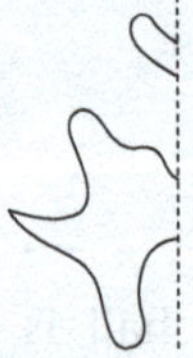

The correct pattern of the other half of the paper will be

(a) 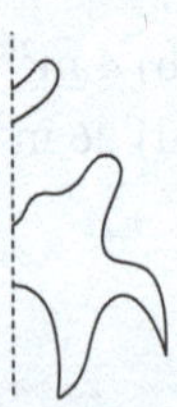

(b) 

(c) Both (a) and (b)

(d) None of these

3. Ms. Bernard drew a series of pictures on the blackboard as shown below

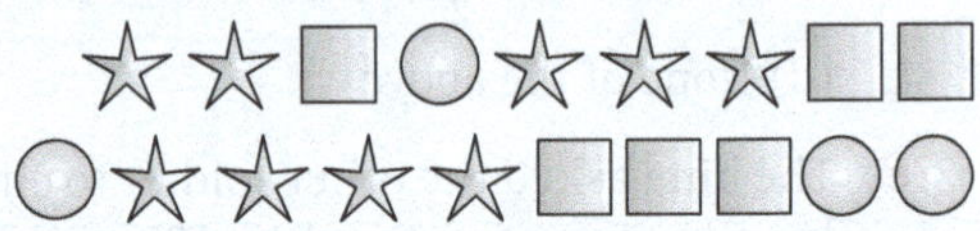

Which of the following options is similar to pattern above?

(a) ABC ABC AABC AAB

(b) AABC AABC AAABBC

(c) AA BC AAABC AAAABC

(d) AABCAAABBCAAAABBBCC

4. The following numbers in the figure '⇩' follows a pattern. Analysis the pattern and find the value of missing number.

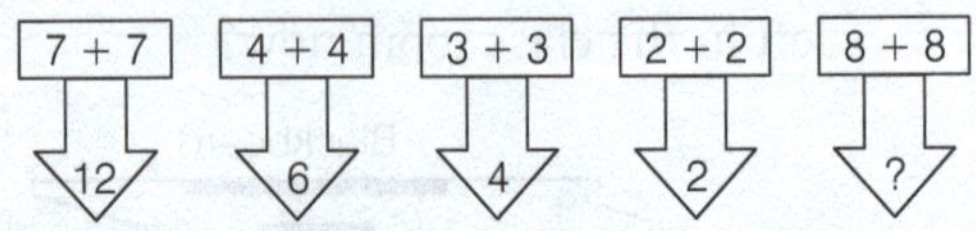

(a) 16 (b) 64 (c) 14 (d) 62

5. What would be the correct next shape for the given pattern?

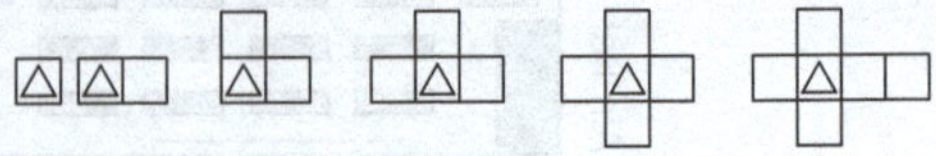

(a) 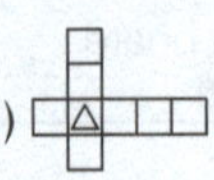

(b) 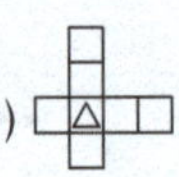

(c) 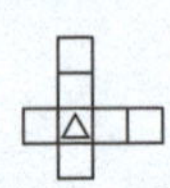

(d) 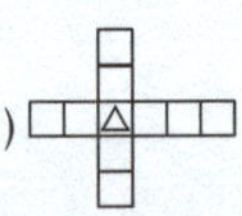

6. If $1 = 0 \times 9 + 1$; $11 = 1 \times 9 + 2$

$111 = 12 \times 9 + 3; 1111 =$ _____ $\times 9 +$ ______

Then, the missing numbers are

(a) 123, 5 (b) 1234, 6
(c) 123, 4 (d) 1234567, 8

7. While arranging her books, Suzane put 3 books on first rack, 6 books on second rack, 12 books on third rack and so on. If she kept the books in the same pattern, then how many books will be kept on fifth rack?

(a) 22 (b) 24 (c) 46 (d) 48

8. While sorting some stationary material Kenya put 58 items in the first box, 69 in the second box, 80 in the third box, 91 in the fourth box and 102 in the fifth box. If this pattern continues, how many items will be their in the 10th box?

(a) 113 (b) 135 (c) 146 (d) 157

9. How many axis/lines of symmetry does the given figure have?

(a) 1 (b) 3
(c) 4 (d) 5

10. How many of the following letters have a vertical line of symmetry

OLYMPIAD

(a) 4 (b) 5
(c) 8 (d) All of these

11. Which of the given below figures will look same on turning a half turn?

(a)  (b)  (c)  (d) 

12. Mr. Gredwick drew four pictures, as shown below.

I. 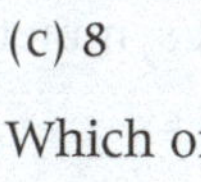 II. 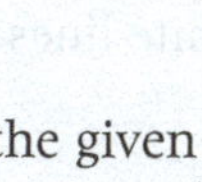 III. 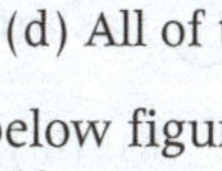 IV. 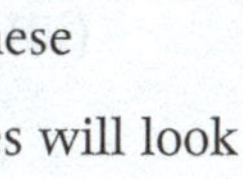

Which figure drawn by Mr. Gredwick is symmetrical about the line.

(a) I (b) I, II (c) III (d) I, III

13. Which of the following letter is symmetrical as pattern of the given figure.

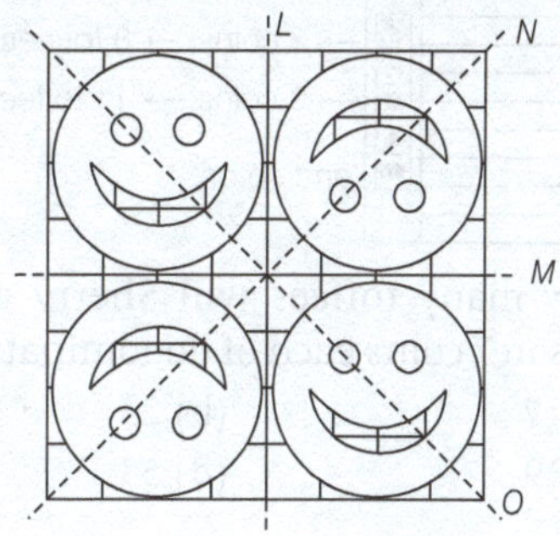

(a) L (b) M
(c) N (d) None of these

14.

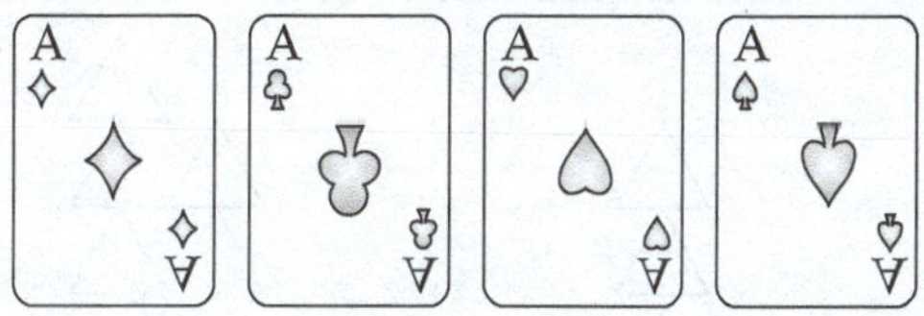

I II III IV

Siddhant while playing with cards placed the above cards on each other while picking up the cards, he turned the pack with half turn and opened each of them one by one.

Which of the above card will look the same after turning half a turn?

(a) II (b) III (c) I (d) IV

15. What is the least number of squares that must be shaded to make the given figure symmetrical about the line *AB*?

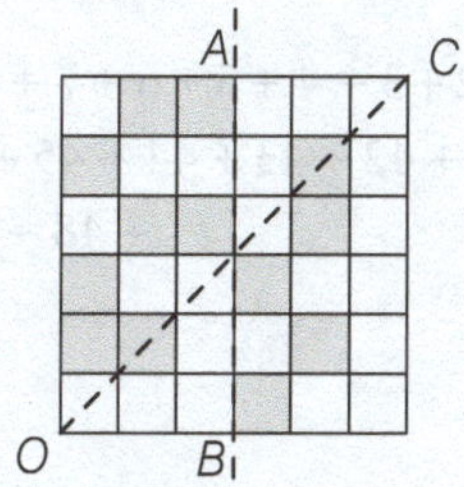

(a) 8 (b) 9 (c) 10 (d) 12

2 Marks Questions

16. In a vending machine a number of toffees come out when coins of denomination of ₹ 5 are put in, as shown below

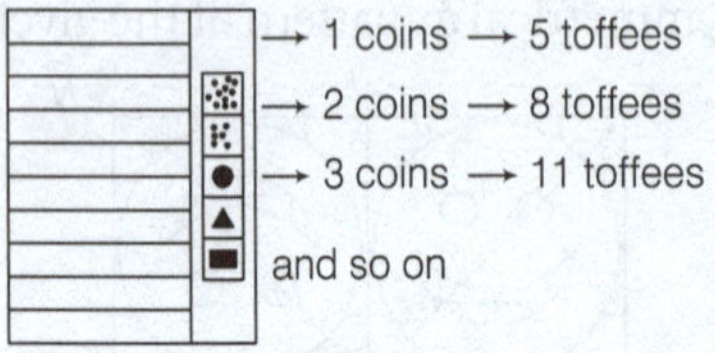

How many toffees will Sherry get, if she puts in 7 coins each of denomination of ₹ 5?

(a) 17 (b) 23
(c) 39 (d) 53

17. Micheal got a homework to draw a pattern of objects.
He drew the following pattern.

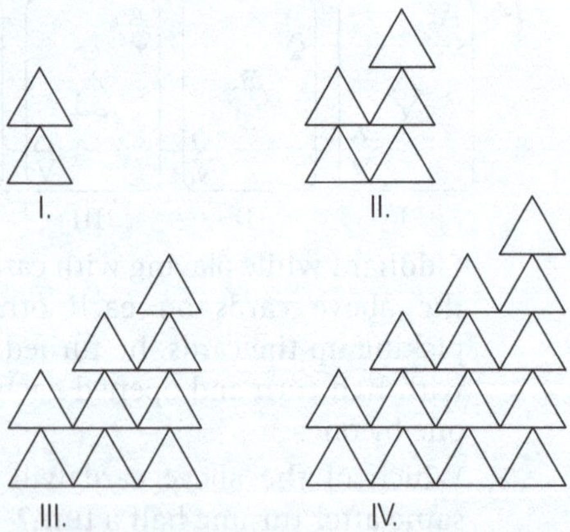

How many total triangles will be used in the last and second last column of the 17th pattern?

(a) 35 (b) 34
(c) 16 (d) 17

18. If $1+2+3+4+5+6+7+8+9=55-10$ and $41+42+43+44+45+46+47+48+49=455-50$, then without actually adding, $91+92+93+94+95+96+97+98+99 = \_\_\_\_$

(a) $999-90$
(b) $995+10$
(c) $955-100$
(d) Cannot be determined

19. What is the smallest number of squares that must be added, so that the line *AB* becomes a line of symmetry?

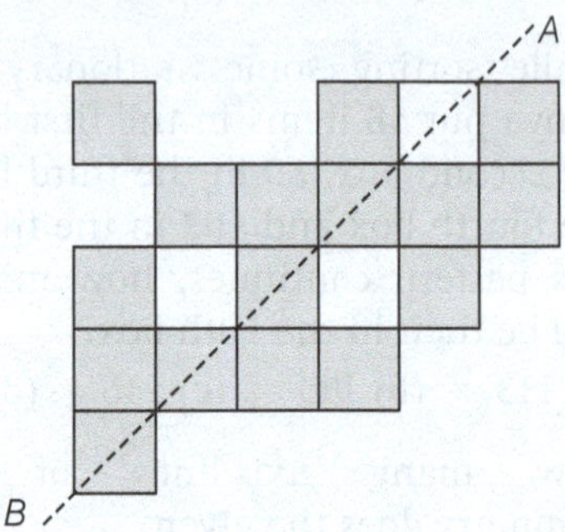

(a) 4 (b) 5
(c) 8 (d) 9

20. State 'T' for true and 'F' for false and select the correct option.

(i) There is no line of symmetry in 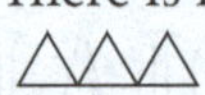

(ii)  has exactly two lines of symmetry

(iii)  has infinite lines of symmetry

	(i)	(ii)	(iii)
(a)	T	F	T
(b)	F	T	F
(c)	T	F	F
(d)	F	T	T

Chapter 11

Data Handling

1 Mark Questions

1. If one full of glass symbol  represents 10 glasses of chocolate milk, then 45 glasses of chocolate milk are represented by

(a) 

(b) 

(c) 

(d) 

2. The pictograph below shows the number of orders completed by Ms. Benrick for her bakery shop.

Number of orders

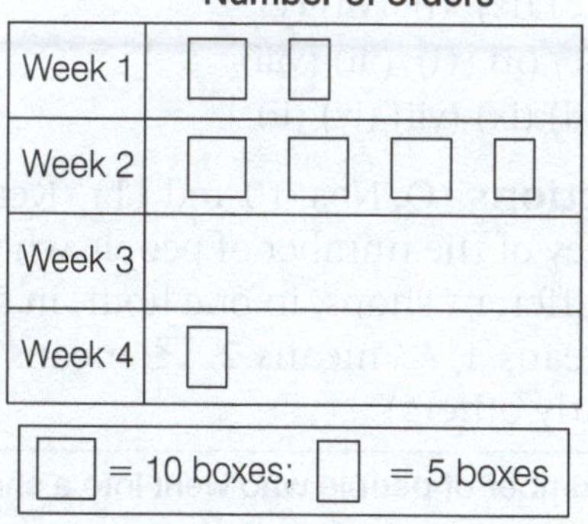

If in week 3, the number of orders completed is 15 less than the number of orders completed in week 2, then which picture would depict the number of orders completed in week 3?

(a) 　(b) 

(c) 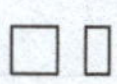　(d) 

3. 50 students go to their schools by different modes as shown in the pictograph. From the pictograph, find how many students does the figure in each key represents?

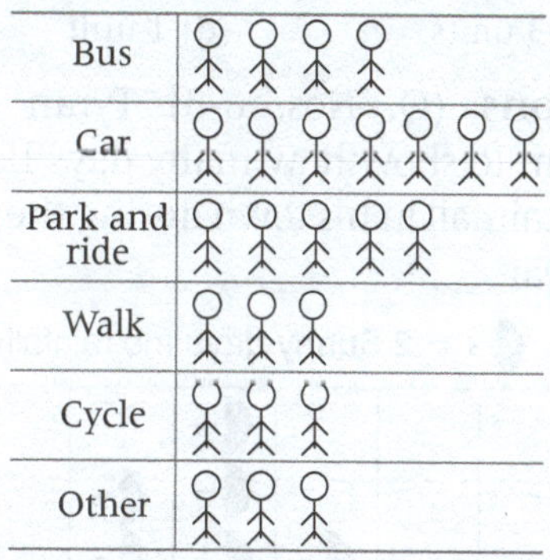

(a)  = 2 students　(b)  = 5 students

(c)  = 10 students　(d) None of these

4. Kristine bakes muffins to sell at her cafe. The pictogram shows the number of muffins she baked on four days.

Number of cakes baked on different days

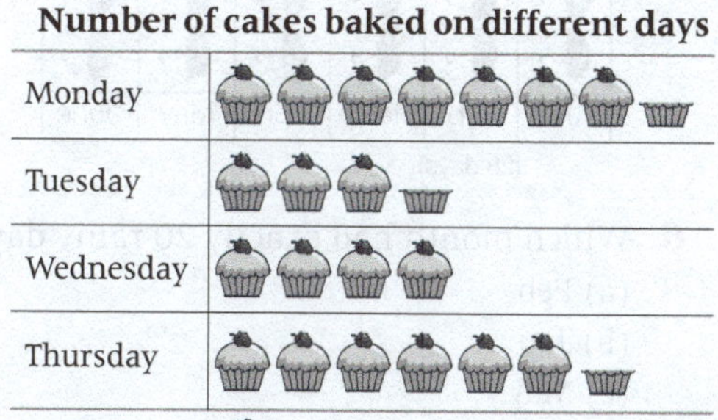

 = 10 muffins  = 5 muffins

What is the total number of muffins she baked?

(a) 200 (b) 190
(c) 215 (d) None of these

5. The graph below shows the length of different nails.

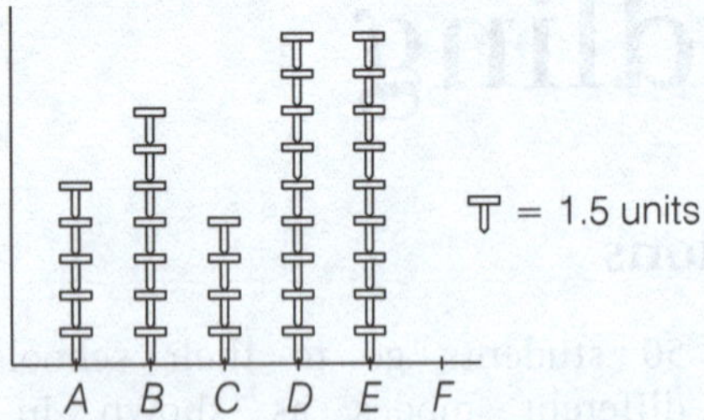

How much longer is the nail *D* than the nail *B* ?

(a) 10.5 units (b) 4.5 units
(c) 3 units (d) 1 unit

Directions (Q. Nos. 6-8) Tyran made a pictogram to show how many days he did not observe rainfall in his town during the first half of the year.

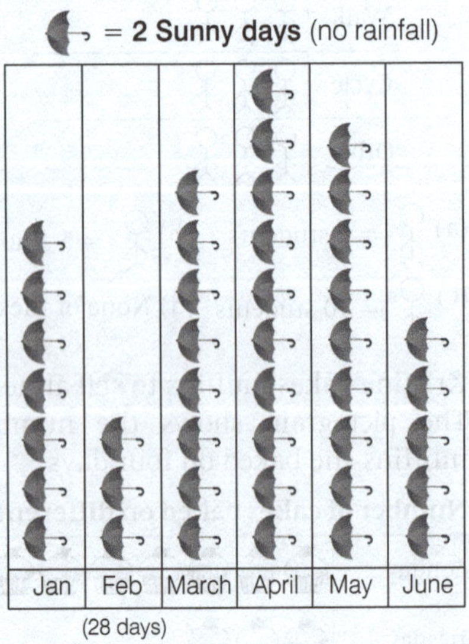

6. Which month had exactly 20 rainy days?

(a) Feb
(b) Jan
(c) May
(d) June

7. How many sunny days were there during the first three months?

(a) 20 (b) 26 (c) 36 (d) 42

8. Which month had the highest number of rainy days?

(a) January (b) June
(c) February (d) March

9. Fill in the blanks and choose the correct option.

(i) 35	(ii) 55	(iii) 140	(iv) 60
(v) 11	(vi) 5 (vii) 6	(viii) 9	(ix) 25

I. If ↓ represents 5 houses, then the number of houses represented by ↓↓↓↓↓ are ....

II. If one symbol △ represents 70 children, then ◺ represents .... children.

III. One ☆ represents .... stars, then 12 such stars represents 72 stars.

IV. If ◇◇ represents 24 people, then........ ◇ such symbols represent 132 people.

I II III IV

(a) (ii) (vii) (ix) (v)
(b) (ix) (i) (vii) (v)
(c) (ii) (vi) (iii) (viii)
(d) (ix) (vii) (iv) (ii)

Directions (Q. Nos. 10 and 11) Kerry did a survey of the number of people who went into different shops, in one hour, in a mall. (if | means 1, ⌐ means 2, ▱ means 5 and similarly others)

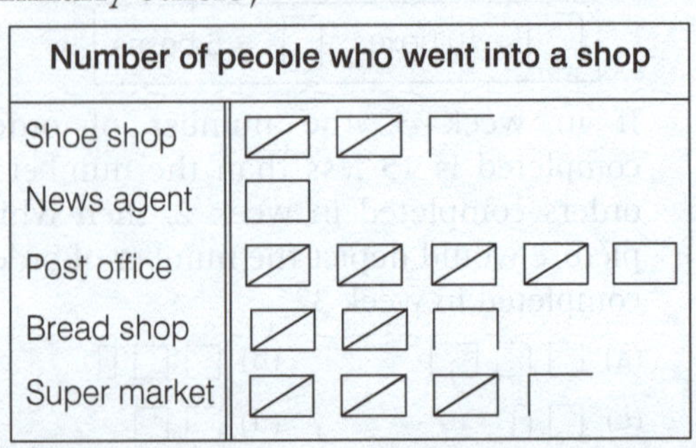

10. How many people went to the super market in one hour?

(a) 17
(b) 18
(c) 13
(d) 3.5

11. How many more people went to the post office than in the shoe shop?

(a) 24
(b) 12
(c) 16
(d) 6

Directions (Q. Nos. 12 and 13) The table given below shows the number of journey a taxi driver made on five days and the charges he took per journey (ride).

Days	Number of journeys	Money collected per ride
Monday	23	₹ 85
Tuesday	36	₹ 112
Wednesday	18	₹ 69
Thursday	31	₹ 124
Friday	35	₹ 109

12. How much money did he collect on the day when he made the most journeys?

(a) ₹4032
(b) ₹3815
(c) ₹4464
(d) None of the above

13. How much more money did he collect on Monday than on Wednesday?

(a) ₹ 1955
(b) ₹ 1242
(c) ₹ 713
(d) ₹ 3197

14. The graph below shows the favourite types of literature of the students of class V (A) and class V (B).

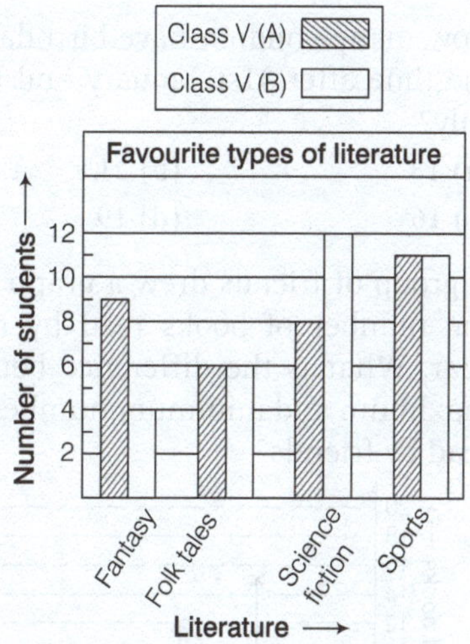

Which type of literature is more preferred by students in class V (A) than in class V (B) and how many students preferred the same?

(a) Sports, 9
(b) Fantasy, 5
(c) Folktales, 4
(d) Science fiction, 3

Directions (Q. Nos. 15 and 16) Ms. Bennet counted the number of students having birthdays in different months of the year.

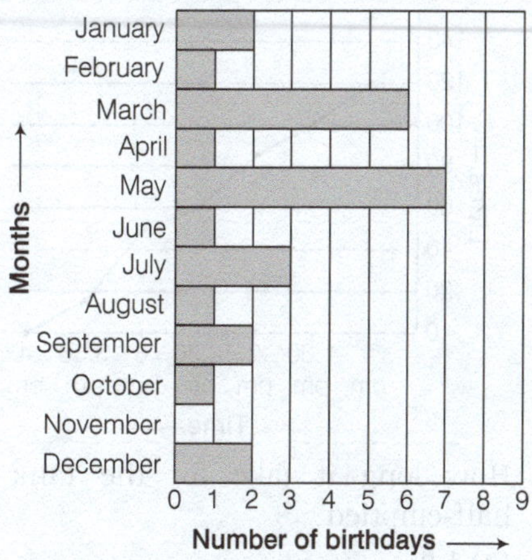

15. In how many months is the number of birthdays greater than 4?

(a) 4 (b) 3
(c) 2 (d) 1

16. How many children have birthdays during the time after 31st January and before 1st July?

(a) 18 (b) 21

(c) 16 (d) 19

17. A group of friends drew a graph depicting the number of books read by them this year. What is the difference between the maximum and minimum number of books read by friends?

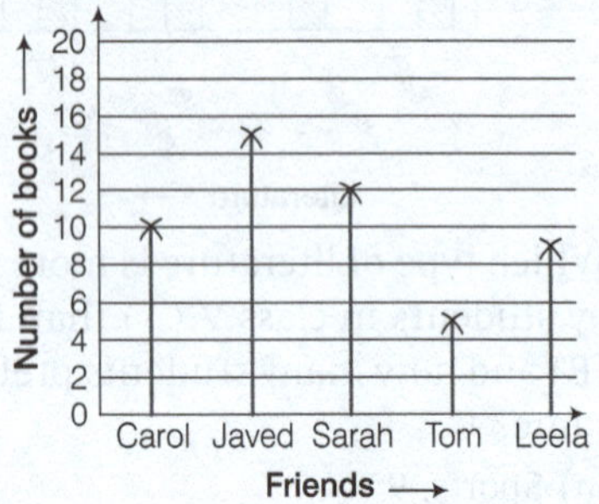

(a) 15 (b) 10

(c) 5 (d) 8

18. A tank was completely filled with water at 1 pm. To empty the tank, water was allowed to flow out at different rate. The line group below shows the volume of water in the tank from 1 pm to 4 pm.

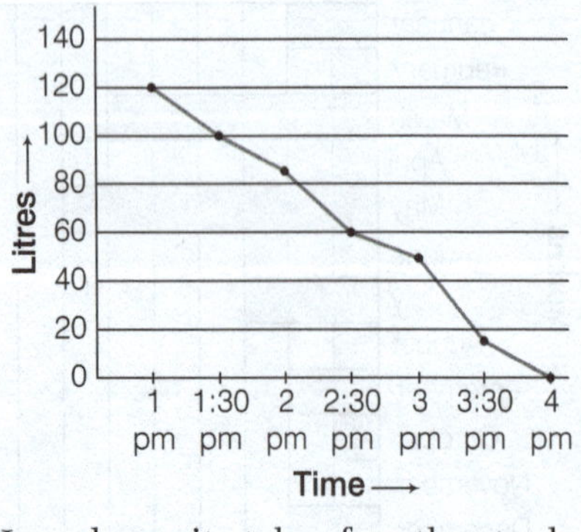

How long it take for the tank to be half-emptied?

(a) 1 h

(b) 1.5 h

(c) 2.5 h

(d) 3 h

Directions (Q. Nos. 19 and 20) Study the line graph given below showing the number of hours, children watch TV in a week and answer the questions that follow.

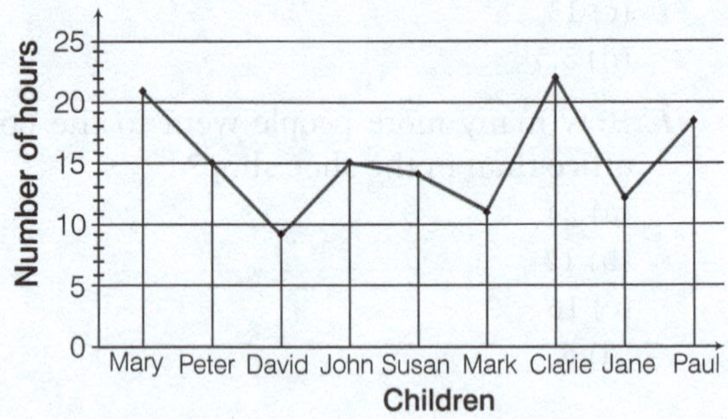

19. Who watched TV fourteen hours a week?

(a) Jane (b) David

(c) Mark (d) Susan

20. What is the difference between the three maximum number of hours and the three minimum number of hours of watching TV?

(a) 45 hours (b) 32 hours

(c) 29 hours (d) 16 hours

Directions (Q. Nos. 21-24) The pie chart shows the number of vehicles in a car park. The total number of vehicles in the car park is 7000. AB is the diameter.

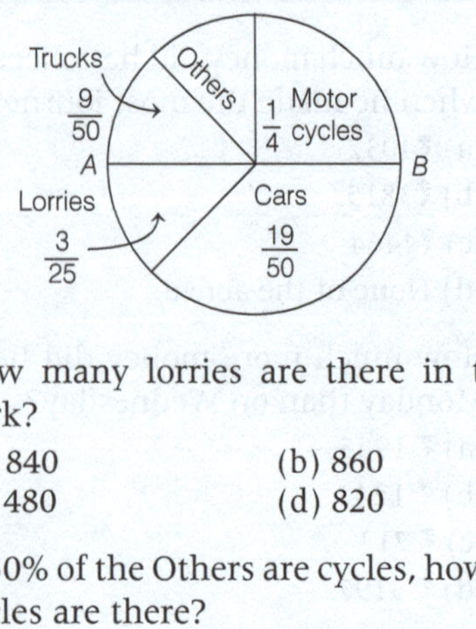

21. How many lorries are there in the car park?

(a) 840 (b) 860

(c) 480 (d) 820

22. If 30% of the Others are cycles, how many cycles are there?

(a) 117 (b) 28

(c) 147 (d) 49

23. What is the ratio of the number of trucks to that of lorries?

(a) 1 : 4
(b) 3 : 2
(c) 3 : 1
(d) 2 : 3

24. How many more cars were parked than motor cycles?

(a) 910
(b) 810
(c) 900
(d) 1010

2 Marks Questions

25. The pictograph shows the distances of cities *A*, *B*, *C* and *D* from city *E*.

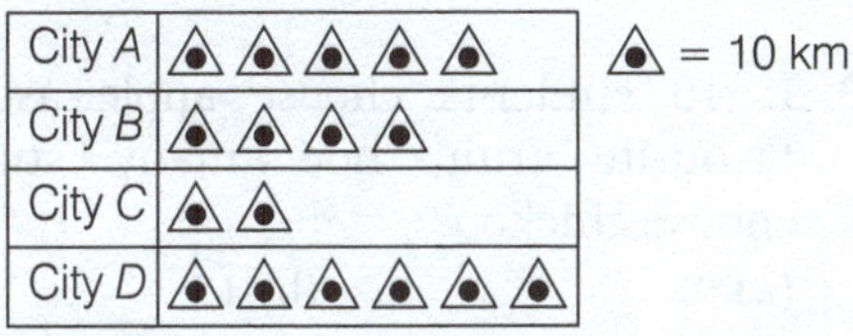

Which of the following road map shows the correct positions of cities A, B, C, D and E?

(a)
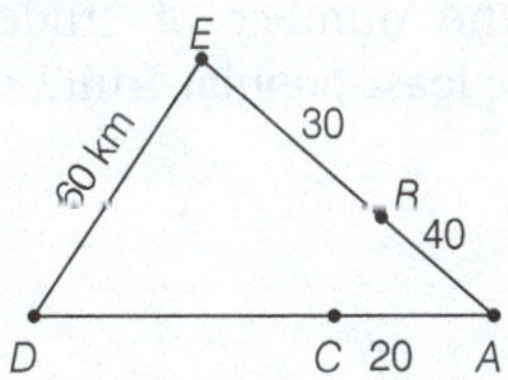

(b)
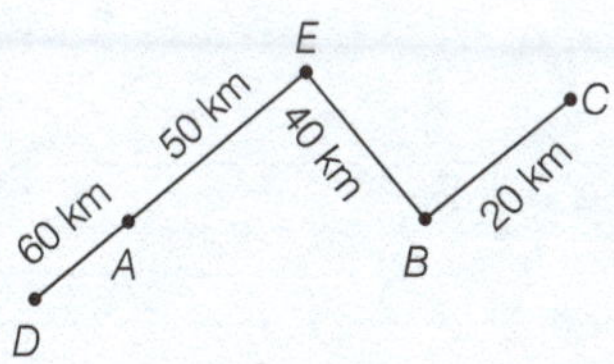

(c)
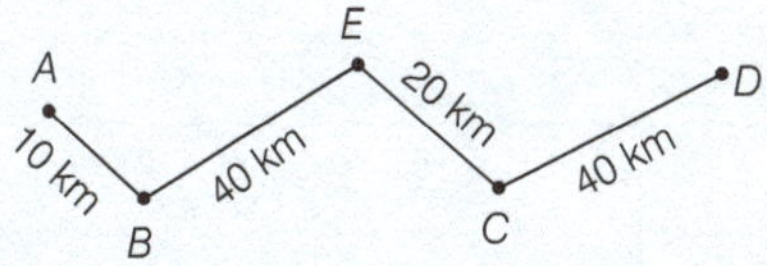

(d)
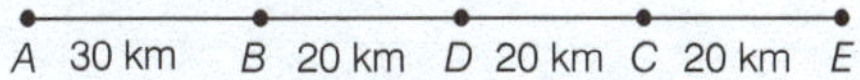

Directions (Q. Nos. 26 and 27) Use the pictograph, showing the number of books read by Sarah, and answer the following questions.

26. Sarah wants to add August's reading to her pictograph. She will use $11\frac{1}{2}$ 📖. How many books did she read in August?

(a) 21
(b) 20
(c) 23
(d) 25

27. Suppose that the legends on scale was changed to "Each 📖 means 4 books". Then, how many books will be drawn to represent the books read in June?

(a) $4\frac{1}{2}$
(b) 4
(c) 5
(d) 10

Directions (Q. Nos. 28 and 29) This graph shows the temperature during mid day on each day in a week.

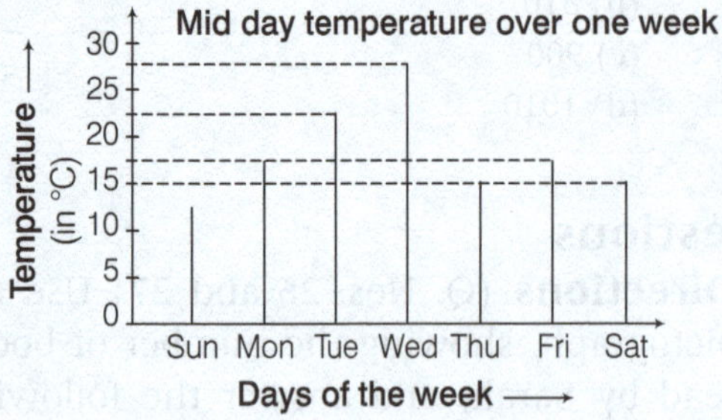

28. How much higher the temperature was on Wednesday than on Saturday?

(a) 15°C
(b) 13.5°C
(c) 13°C
(d) 12.5°C

29. On which day was the temperature between 27°C and 18°C?

(a) Tuesday
(b) Monday
(c) Friday
(d) Wednesday

Directions (Q. Nos. 30 and 31) Students of class 5 were asked to choose their favourite fruit. The given pie chart shows their choices.

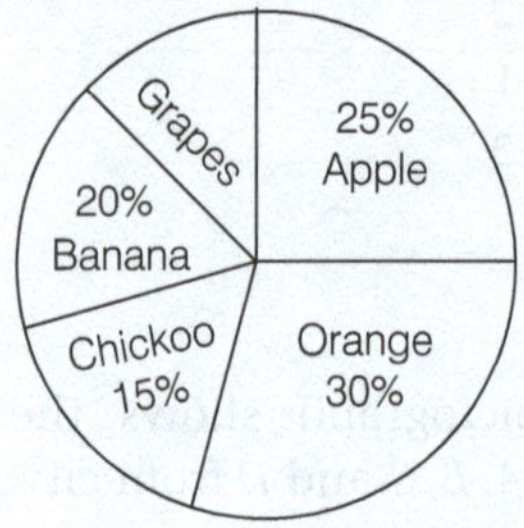

30. If 10 students choose apple as their favourite fruit, how many students choose chickoo?

(a) 9 (b) 15
(c) 6 (d) 8

31. What is the ratio of the number of students who choose the most popular fruit to the number of students who choose the least popular fruit?

(a) 5 : 2
(b) 2 : 5
(c) 1 : 3
(d) 3 : 1

PRACTICE SET 01

1 Mark Questions

1. One of the puzzle is given in the figure having different types of angle formed. Which of the angle marked is an obtuse angle?

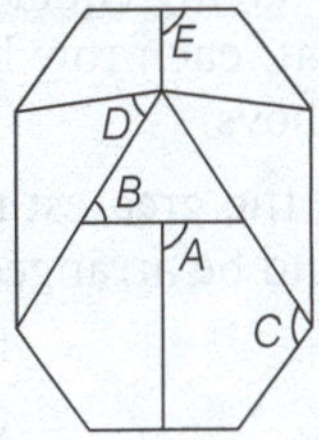

(a) A (b) B (c) D (d) C

2. On the basis of arrangement given below, the value of missing number is

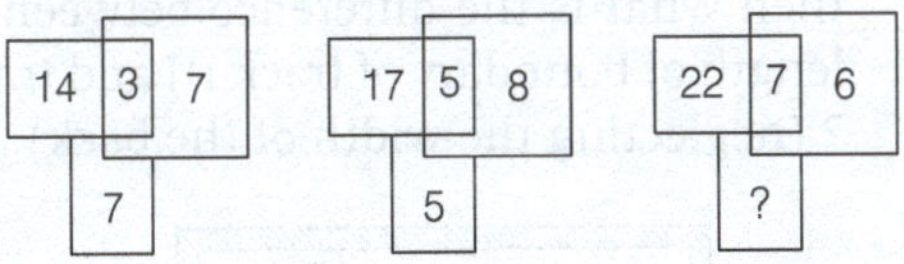

(a) 3 (b) 4 (c) 7 (d) 6

3. What is the total number of cubes in the given figure?

(a) 13 (b) 15 (c) 18 (d) 25

4. How many such triangles must be shaded to make AB as the line of symmetry?

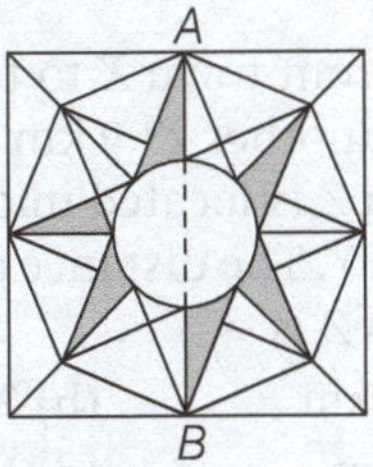

(a) 2 (b) 3 (c) 4 (d) 5

5. The line graph given below shows how the group of pupils go to office

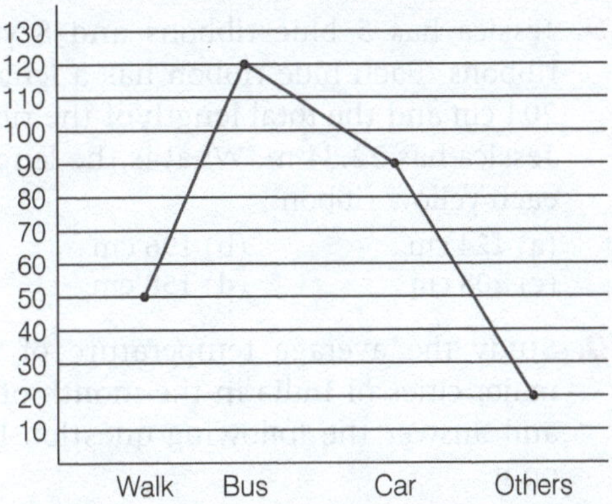

The fraction of the pupils go to office by car is

(a) $\frac{3}{28}$ (b) $\frac{9}{28}$ (c) $\frac{9}{22}$ (d) $\frac{3}{7}$

6. If

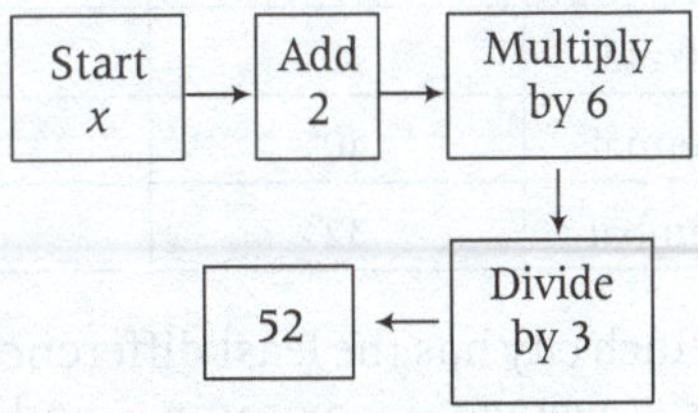

Then, the starting number is

(a) 12 (b) 18
(c) 48 (d) 36

7. Which net would make a cube where no two faces having same alphabet meet to form an edge?

(a)
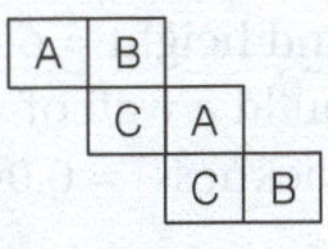

(b)
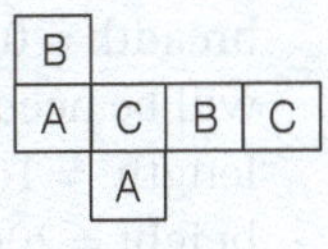

(c)
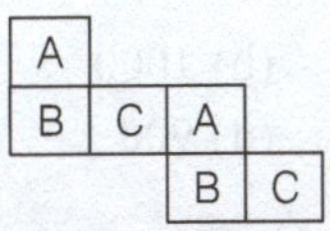

(d)
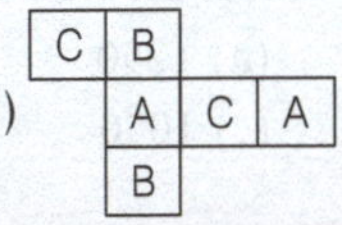

8. There was 15 kg of flour in bag *A*. After some flour was transferred from bag *A* to bag *B*, there was 3 kg more flour in bag *A* than in bag *B*, then there was 8 kg of flour in bag *B*. How much flour was transferred from bag *A* to bag *B*?

(a) 7 kg (b) 4 kg
(c) 2 kg (d) 11 kg

9. Jessica has 5 blue ribbons and 8 yellow ribbons. Each blue ribbon has a length of 204 cm and the total length of the ribbons Jessica has 22.84 m. What is the length of each yellow ribbon?

(a) 124 cm (b) 196 cm
(c) 208 cm (d) 158 cm

10. Study the average temperature of some major cities of India in the month of May and answer the following question based on it.

City	Average maximum temperature (in °C)	Average minimum temperature (in °C)
New Delhi	38°	32°
Kolkata	39°	27°
Chennai	40°	28°
Mumbai	32°	28°

Which city has the least difference between its average maximum and average minimum temperature?

(a) Chennai
(b) New Delhi
(c) Mumbai
(d) Kolkata

11. How many bricks of length = 0.2 m, breadth = 0.08 m and height = 6 cm, will be needed to build a wall of length = 10 m, thickness = 0.06 m and height = 200 cm?

(a) 1250 (b) 1000
(c) 1050 (d) 900

12. The table shows the number of children in the school playground.

Playground

Children	Number
Girls	144
Boys	128

The teacher plans to arrange the children in rows having equal number of children such that, each row has either only girls or only boys.

What is the greatest number of students that could be arranged in each row?

(a) 12 (b) 16
(c) 24 (d) 32

13. Susan, Laden, John run on different tracks of a rectangular field. If the dimensions of the tracks are given below, then what is the difference between the length of boundary of track III and track I ? (neglecting the width of the back)

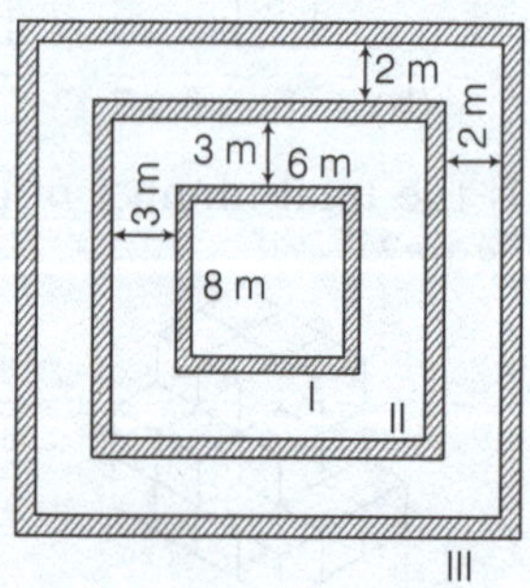

(a) 68 m (b) 40 m
(c) 24 m (d) 16 m

14. At 10 : 30 am, Tracy completed $\frac{5}{6}$ of her journey from town *X* to town *Y*. She had to travel another 23.9 km to reach town *Y* and town *Z* is located mid way of town *X* and town *Y*. The distance between town X and town *Z* is

(a) 143.4 km (b) 28.64 km
(c) 71.7 km (d) None of these

15. The amount of money Jack had $\frac{2}{5}$ as much as Kerry's. After Jack received ₹ 12.40 from Kerry, Jack had $\frac{3}{4}$ as much money as Kerry. How much more money should Kerry give to Jack, so that the boys would have an equal amount of money?

(a) ₹ 54 (b) ₹ 56
(c) ₹ 68 (d) None of these

16. What number is it?

I. It is a two-digit number.

II. Its unit digit is 1 subtracted from $2 \times (2 \div 2)$.

III. Its ten's digit is 15 subtracted from 36 and then divided by 7.

(a) 42 (b) 13 (c) 81 (d) 31

17. Fill in the blanks using the appropriate options from the box given.

(i) 47	(ii) XXVII
(iii) 3	(iv) $100 + 20$
(v) 9	(vi) XXXV
(vii) 100×20	(viii) $100 \div 20$
(ix) units and tens	
(x) tens and hundred	
(xi) units, tens and hundred	

I. A number is divisible by 9, if the sum of the digits of the number is divisible by ______.

II. XI + XVI + XX = ______

III. If there are 100 toffees in a packet, then the number of toffees in 20 such bags is ______.

IV. A number is divisible by 8, if the number formed by the digits in ______ places is divisible by 8.

	I	II	III	IV
(a)	(v)	(vi)	(viii)	(x)
(b)	(iii)	(i)	(iv)	(ix)
(c)	(v)	(i)	(vii)	(xi)
(d)	(iii)	(vi)	(viii)	(x)

18. Miranda counted to 60 using multiple of 6. Her friends concluded the following statements:

Lara: They all are odd numbers.

Duke: They all have 6 in the ones place.

Chrish: They can all be divided evenly by 3.

Jack: They can all be divided by 12.

Who said the correct statement?

(a) Lara (b) Duke
(c) Chrish (d) Jack

19. After every nineth visit to a restaurant, Saran receives a free beverage. After every twelfth visit she receives a free appetiser. On which visit will she receive a free beverage and a free appetiser both?

(a) 12th (b) 27th (c) 36th (d) 48th

20. A rectangular sheet of some perimeter is to be cut into smaller pieces of equal size. It can be cut out into three types of same sized sheets of the following sizes.

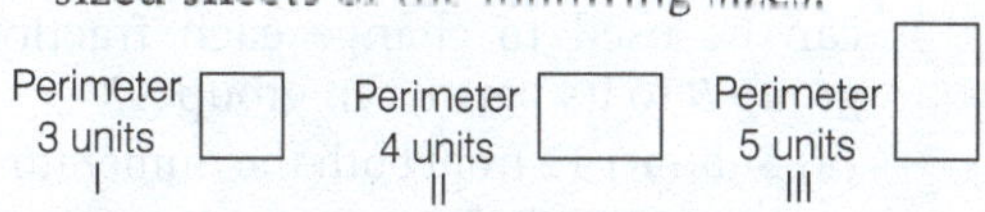

What can be the least perimeter of the larger rectangular sheet from which above smaller sheets can be cut out?

(a) 40 units (b) 45 units
(c) 50 units (d) 60 units

21. State 'T' for true and 'F' for false and choose the correct option.

I. '1' is a factor of every number.

II. '0' is neither prime nor composite.

III. LCM of two numbers = Product of number × HCF.

IV. HCF of two coprime numbers is 0.

	I	II	III	IV
(a)	F	T	F	T
(b)	T	F	T	F
(c)	F	F	T	T
(d)	T	T	F	F

22. 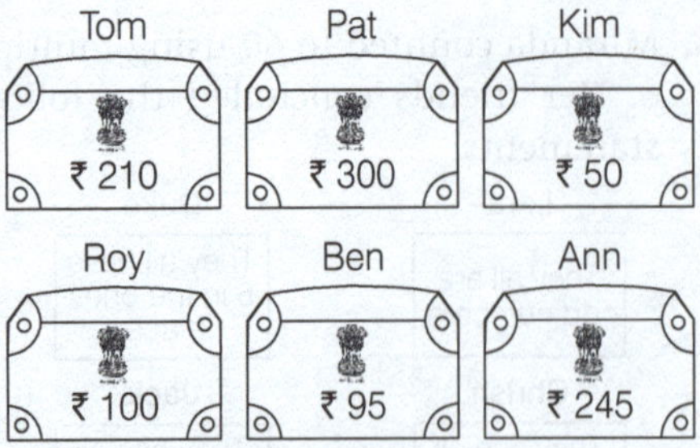

Six friends save money for an orphanage to donate on occasion of children's day. Find who saved 1/20th of the total amount saved by all the friends.

(a) Kim (b) Pat
(c) Ben (d) Roy

23. The chart shows two sets of fractions. Each fraction in group *A* is paired with an equivalent fraction in group *B*.

Group *A*	Group *B*
28/36	7/9
12/20	3/5
16/28	4/7

Which of these describes the method that can be used to change each fraction in group *B* to its partner in group *A*?

(a) Subtract 12 from both the numerator and the denominator
(b) Subtract 26 from both the numerator and the denominator
(c) Multiply both the numerator and the denominator by 4
(d) Divide both the numerator and denominator by 2/4

24. Christen uses a cup and a jar to mix juice. It takes 3 cups of juice to fill in the jar.
He pours pineapple juice into the jar until it is half full. Then, he adds half a cup of orange juice. How full is the jar now?

(a) One-quarter full (b) Two-third full
(c) Three-fourth full (d) None of these

25. Six friends collected sugar for the cake competition to be held next day. Arrange these bags according to their weight from the lightest to the heaviest and choose the correct option.

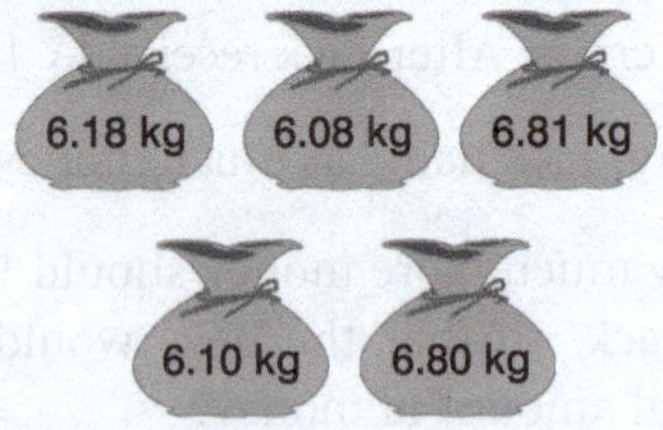

(a) 6.18 < 6.08 < 6.81 < 6.10 < 6.80
(b) 6.08 < 6.10 < 6.18 < 6.80 < 6.81
(c) 6.10 < 6.18 < 6.08 < 6.80 < 6.81
(d) None of the above

Directions (Q. Nos. 26 and 27) The table given below shows the mass of children when they were born.

Children	Mass (in kg)
Emma	4.65
Joy	3.75
Zua	5.25
Tim	3.59
Luca	4.96

26. What is the difference in mass of Emma and Zua?

(a) 0.50 kg (b) 600 g
(c) 750 g (d) 1 kg

27. The total mass of Joy and Luca together is

(a) 9.01 kg (b) 8 kg
(c) 8.50 kg (d) 8.71 kg

28. Stephanie's stacked toy blocks to form the shape as shown below:

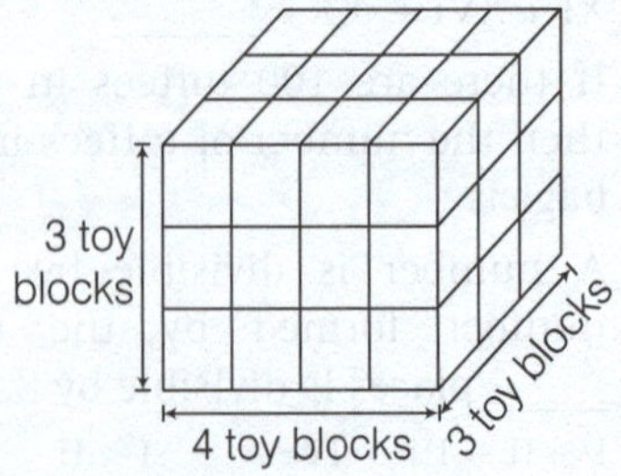

How many toy blocks are in Stephanie's stack of toy blocks?

(a) 12 (b) 24 (c) 36 (d) 48

29. Two cubical boxes are dipped into two same types of vessels having equal quantity of water as shown below

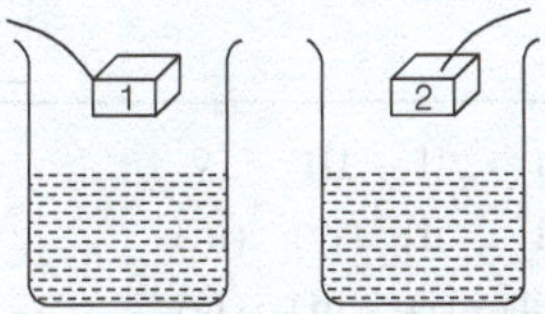

If the dimensions of box 1 is 2 cm × 3 cm × 4 cm and of box 2 is 3.5 cm × 1.5 cm × 0.05 m, then in which of the given vessels will the water raise to more height?

(a) Both the box will have same height of raised water

(b) Box 2

(c) Box 1

(d) Cannot be determined

30. Triangles are rigid strong structures used for rafters in buildings and curved domes. Engineers use this shape in making bridges. One of them is given in the picture below

The bridge is made up of same type of angles as shown below

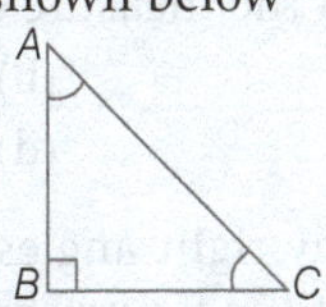

If one angle is right angle and the other two angles are equal, then the sum of the measure of the other two angles is

(a) 30° (b) 45° (c) 60° (d) 90°

31. Points P, Q, R, S and T lie on a polygon as shown below

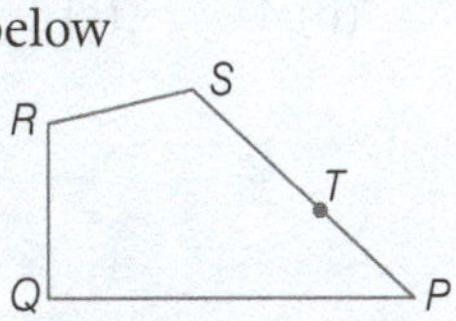

Which of the following tables classified the angles of the polygon correctly?

(a)

Angle	Type
P	Obtuse
Q	Straight
R	Acute
S	Acute
T	Right

(b)

Angle	Type
P	Acute
Q	Right
R	Obtuse
S	Obtuse
T	Straight

(c)

Angle	Type
P	Acute
Q	Straight
R	Obtuse
S	Right
T	Right

(d)

Angle	Type
P	Acute
Q	Straight
R	Obtuse
S	Obtuse
T	Right

32.

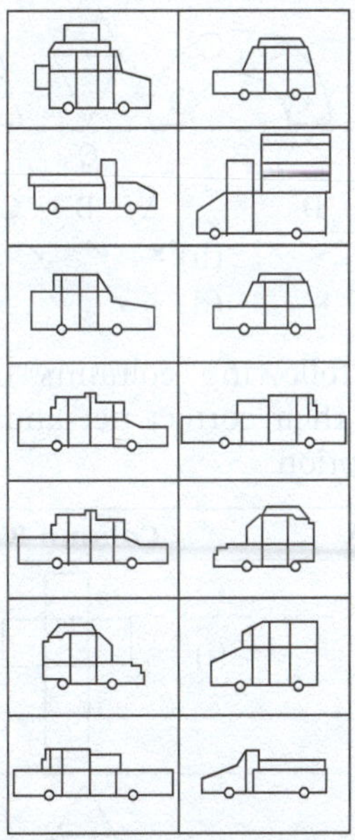

The above parking lot has a fixed space of 2 m × 1 m for each car to be parked. Then, the total area of the parking lot is

(a) 28 sq m (b) 27 sq m

(c) 11 sq m (d) 36 sq m

33. A basketball match is to be held next week at South hall united. For this, the floor of the basketball court is to be painted. If 2 L of paint is needed to paint 150 sq ft of the court. Then, how much paint is required to complete the painting of floor?

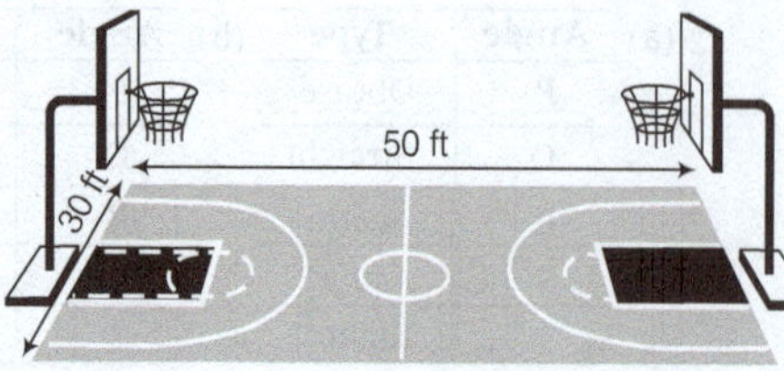

(a) 10 L (b) 20 L
(c) 200 L (d) 150 L

34. If a cross (×) and a tick (✓) is marked on the figures that are symmetrical and non-symmetrical respectively, then choose the correct option on the basis of it.

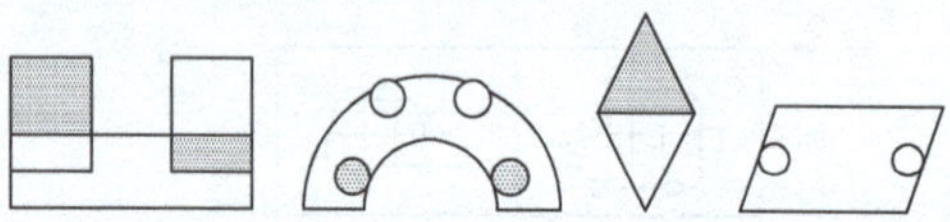

	A	B	C	D
(a)	✓	×	×	✓
(b)	×	✓	✓	✓
(c)	×	×	×	×
(d)	✓	✓	✓	✓

35. Match the following columns of solid shapes with their correct net and choose the correct option.

Column A		Column B	
I.	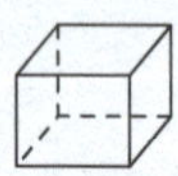	(i)	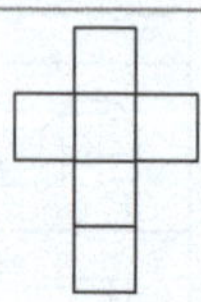
II.	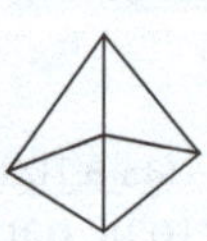	(ii)	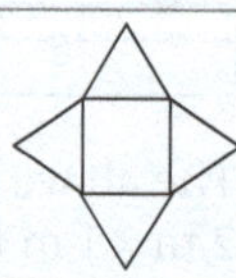
III.	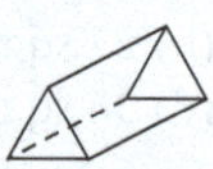	(iii)	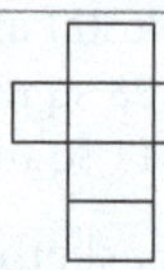
IV.	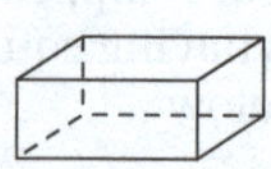	(iv)	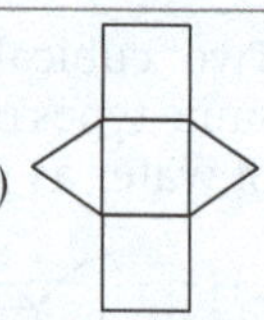

	I	II	III	IV
(a)	(i)	(ii)	(iv)	(iii)
(b)	(ii)	(i)	(iii)	(iv)
(c)	(iv)	(iii)	(i)	(ii)

(d) None of the above

36. A number when rounded off to the nearest thousands becomes 18000. Which of the following could be the number?

(a) 17475 (b) 18975
(c) 17675 (d) 18675

37. 9th multiple of 19 is ...... more than the 7th multiple of 17.

(a) 52 (b) 62
(c) 72 (d) 42

38. Julee birthday party starts at 11 : 20 am. and finished 3 h 30 min later. When did the party finish?

(a) 3 : 50 pm (b) 1 : 50 pm
(c) 2 : 50 am (d) 2 : 50 pm

39. If sum of three angles of a quadrilateral is 290°, find the measure of the 4th angle.

(a) 90° (b) 80°
(c) 70° (d) 100°

40. How many right angles are there on the outside of the figure shown below?

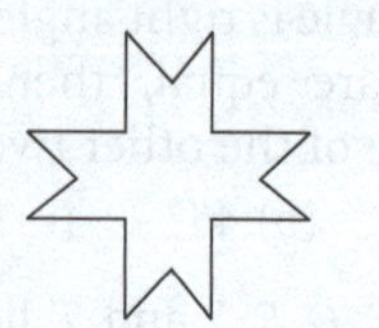

(a) 2 (b) 4 (c) 1 (d) 3

2 Marks Questions

41. On the basis of the given block, find the missing numbers.

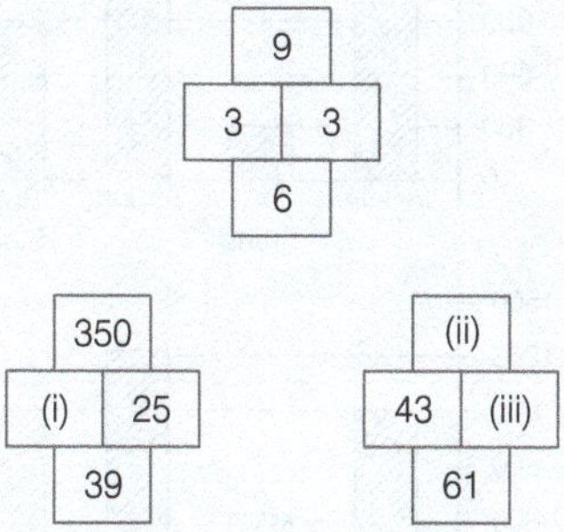

	(i)	(ii)	(iii)		(i)	(ii)	(iii)
(a)	70	1120	16	(b)	35	690	19
(c)	14	774	18	(d)	18	1170	65

42. Miss. Julia went for shopping to buy a pair of jeans, a black shirt and a brown bag. The cost of these things at different shops are given below

	Jeans	Shirt	Bag
Shop 1	₹ 1147.21	₹ 534.23	₹ 520.12
Shop 2	₹ 1272.46	₹ 324.49	₹ 420.41
Shop 3	₹ 1014.76	₹ 576.23	₹ 500.29

From which shop shall she buy the things to have a minimum bill of the items, considering that she buys all the items from one shop only?

(a) Shop 1

(b) Shop 2

(c) Shop 3

(d) Cannot be determined

43. For every 220 mL of lemon juice, a drink seller mixes it with 770 mL of water to make lemonade. The drink seller has 2 bottles of lemon juice. Each bottle contains 1100 mL of lemon juice. How much lemonade can he make?

(a) 9 L 900 mL (b) 9009 mL

(c) 9.9 mL (d) None of these

44.

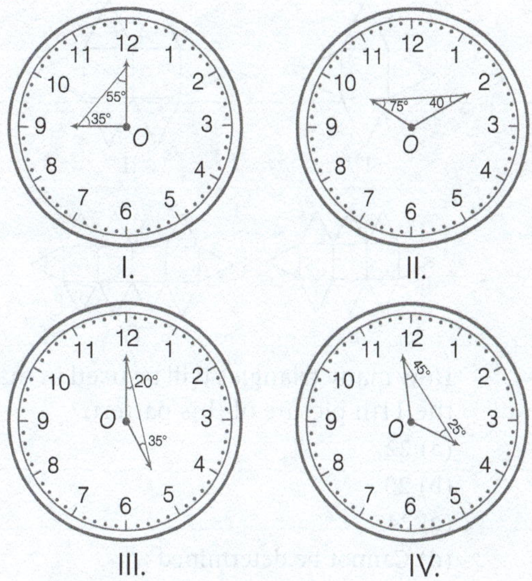

The clocks given in figures show different time. On the basis of it, different angles are formed between the hour hand and the minute hand.

Find the angle formed between the hands and choose the correct option.

(a) 90°, 75°, 130°, 115°

(b) 90°, 65°, 125°, 110°

(c) 100°, 50°, 135°, 80°

(d) None of the above

45. In the given figure, a window is fixed at the centre part of the wall. Find the cost of painting a wall of 15 m long and 12 m wide, if the cost of painting is ₹ 50 per 100 m^2?

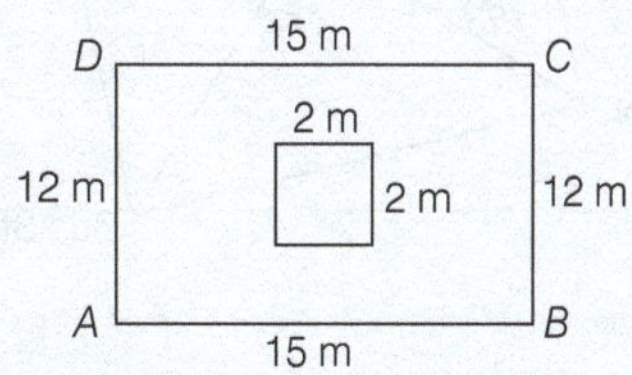

(a) ₹ 88 (b) ₹ 120

(c) ₹ 160 (d) ₹ 180

46. Martin used triangles and squares to draw a series of pictures as shown below

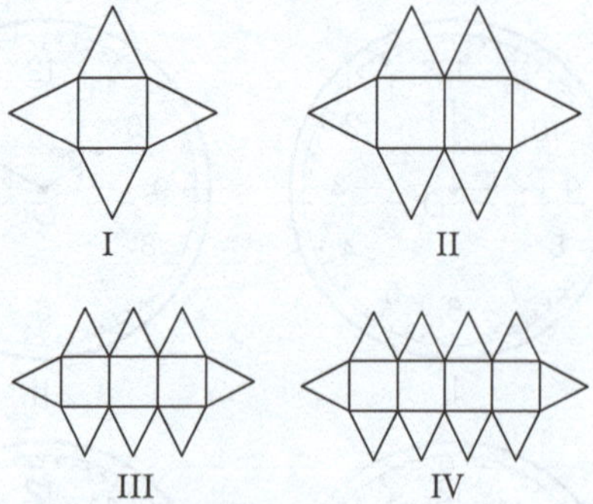

How many triangles will be used in making the 11th picture of this pattern?

(a) 22

(b) 20

(c) 24

(d) Cannot be determined

47. How many of the following digits have atleast one line of symmetry?

01234567

(a) No one (b) 1

(c) 2 (d) 3

48. Eyon makes a figure which shows the distance of some important places from his house.

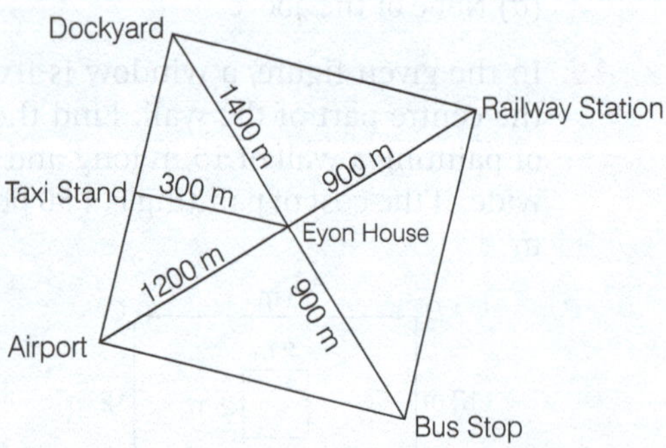

Which one of the following bar graphs is correct for the above given picture?

(a)

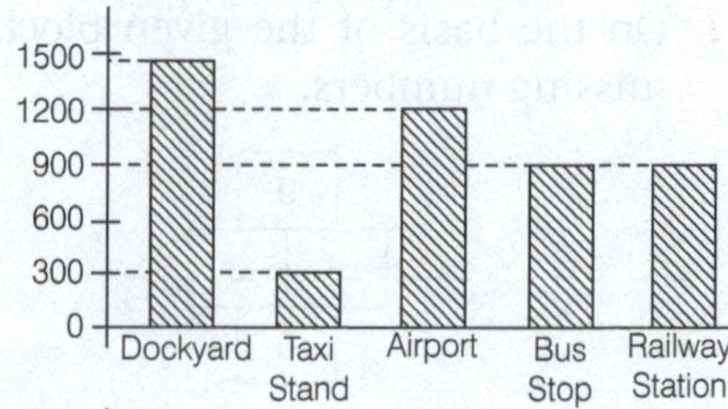

(b)

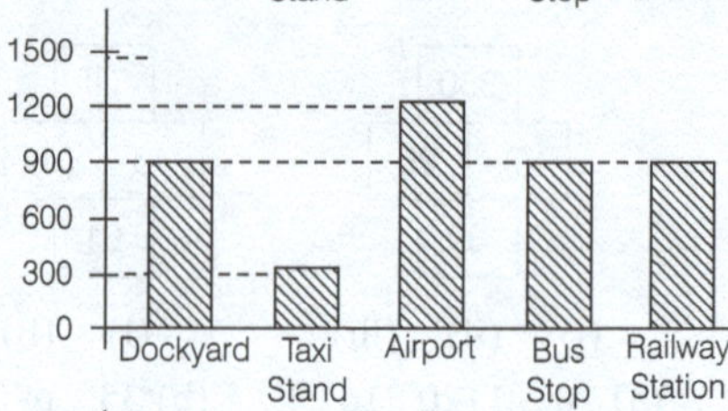

(c)

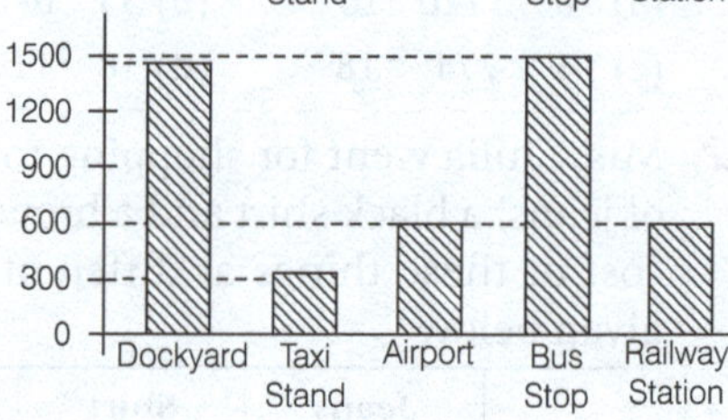

(d) None of the above

49. There are 160 students in a class $\left(\frac{3}{8}\right)$ of them are boys of which $\frac{1}{3}$ wear bracelet. $\left(\frac{4}{5}\right)$ of the girls wear bracelet. How many students wear bracelet?

(a) 120 (b) 100 (c) 80 (d) 60

50. Renu joint two square shape boxes to each others and get a new figure. Each side of square boxes is 5 cm. Find the area of new figure.

(a) 50 cm^2 (b) 25 cm^2

(c) 100 cm^2 (d) None of these

PRACTICE SET 02

1 Mark Questions

1. Following the given pattern, find the value of '$C + D$'.

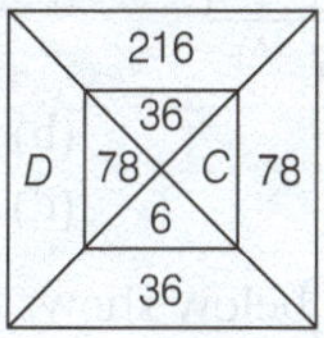

(a) 486 (b) 481
(c) 468 (d) None of these

2. 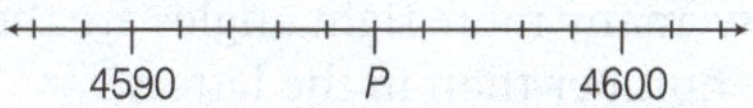

From above figure, subtracting P from 71099 and rounding off the result to the nearest thousand will give

(a) 66500 (b) 66505
(c) 67000 (d) 70000

3. Karen went running 3 times this week. Each time, she ran 2.5 mile. Which number line has point K graphed, so that it best represents the total distance (in mile) Karen ran?

(a) 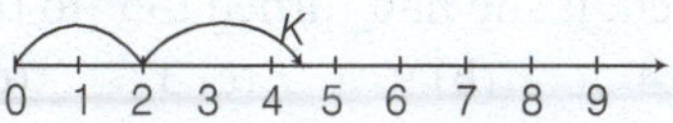

(b) 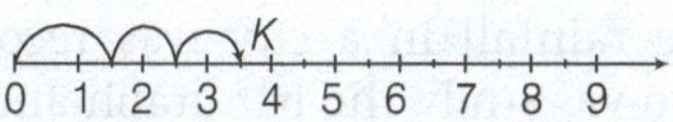

(c) 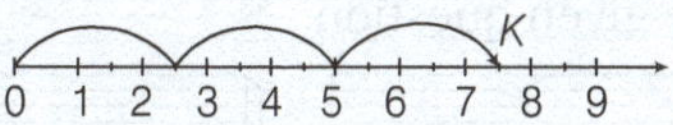

(d) 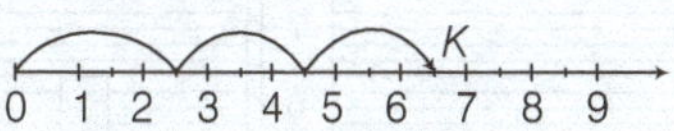

4. What is the area of the shaded part of the figure below?

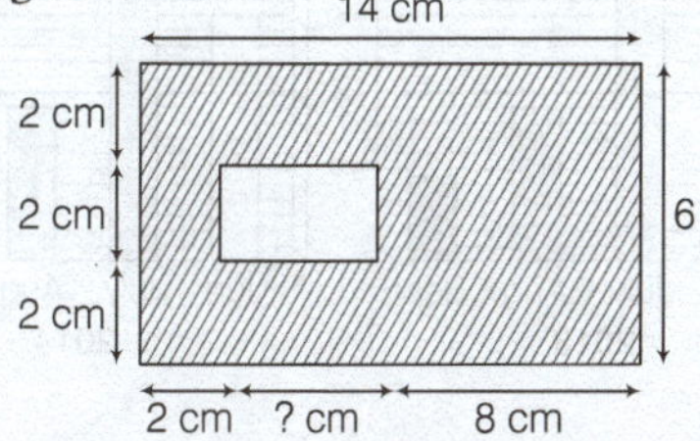

(a) 68 cm^2 (b) 72 cm^2
(c) 76 cm^2 (d) 80 cm^2

5. Given,  – 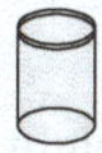 = 50 g

 –  = 20 g

If total weight of ,  and  is 240 g, then what is the weight of ?

(a) 100 g (b) 110 g (c) 50 g (d) 90 g

6. Janellia has an aquarium in the shape of a cube with edges 3 cm each. She started arranging cubes with edges 1 cm each inside the aquarium in the way you can see in the picture. Atmost how many more such cubes can Janellia put into the aquarium?

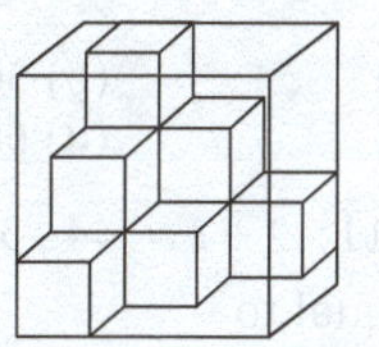

(a) 9 (b) 13 (c) 17 (d) 27

7. Anita was studying the ancient number system of Aryan people. She made following table on the basis of it.

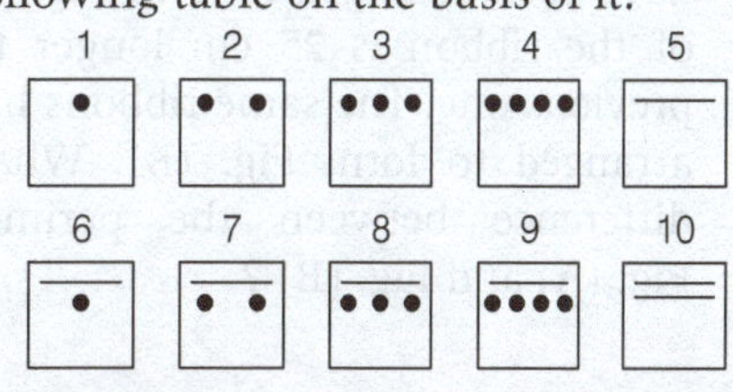

What is the symbol for 19 on the basis of given system of numbers?

(a) 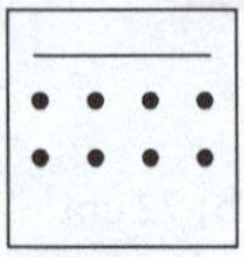

(b) 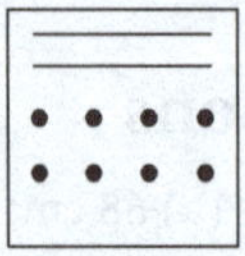

(c) 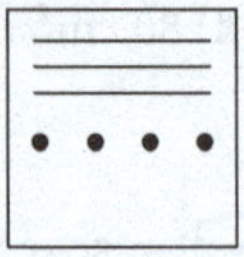

(d) 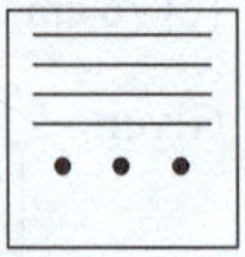

8. Boxes of height 12 inch are being stacked next to boxes that are 18 inch in height. What is the shortest height at which the two stacks of boxes will be of the same height?

(a) 2.4 inch (b) 36 inch

(c) 72 inch (d) 12 inch

9.

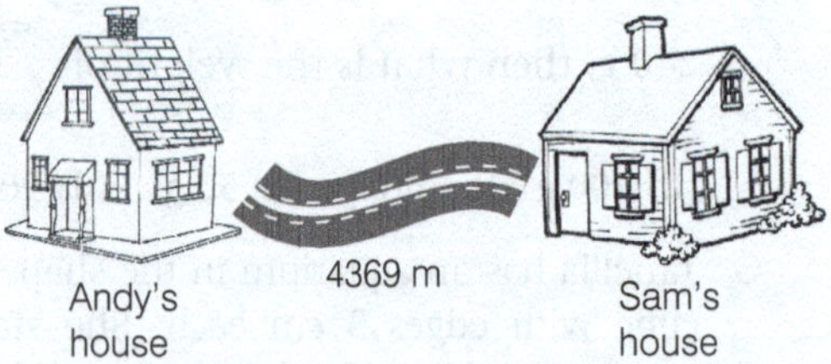

The difference of distance between Andy's and Sam's house rounding to the nearest hundred metre and to nearest thousand metres is

(a) 200 m (b) 369 m

(c) 400 m (d) 600 m

10. If $1+1=11$; $2+2=44$; $3+4=916$, then $4+5$ is equal to

(a) 99 (b) 1818

(c) 1625 (d) None of these

11. Four paper ribbons of uniform width 10 cm have been arranged to form Fig. (A). Each of the ribbon is 25 cm longer than the previous one. The same ribbons have been arranged to form Fig. (B). What is the difference between the perimeters of Fig. (A) and Fig. (B) ?

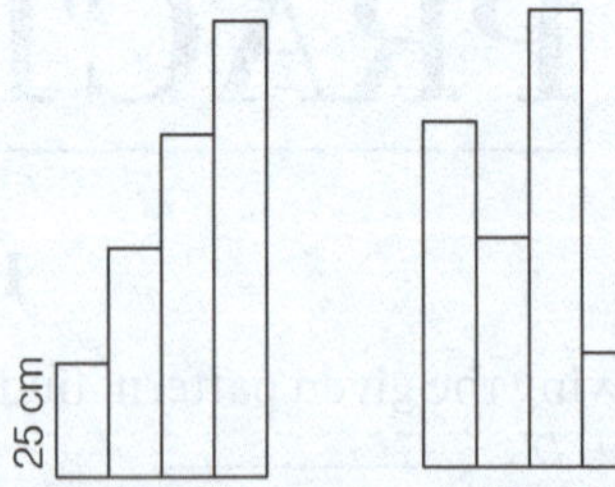

Fig. (A) Fig. (B)

(a) 10 cm (b) 20 cm

(c) 40 cm (d) 50 cm

12. The figure below shows a date.

How many more right angles are there in the number than in the letters?

(a) 6 (b) 10

(c) 16 (d) 20

13.

1	2	3
4	5	6
7	8	9

↑ Facing

Shimpy was standing on box 5. After she made a 270° turn to the right (clockwise), she faced box 4. Which number would she faced, if she had turned 135° to the left?

(a) 4 (b) 9 (c) 3 (d) 7

14. The rainfall in a city was recorded for Two yr. Study the bar graph and answer the given question.

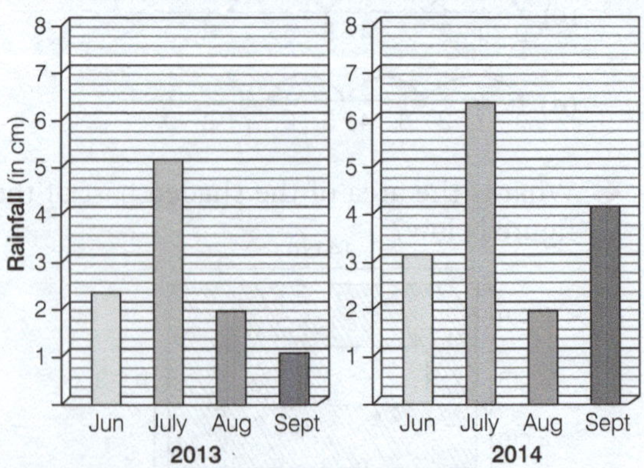

How much more rainfall was recorded in July 2014 compared to August 2013?

(a) 1.2 cm (b) 4.4 cm
(c) 7.0 cm (d) None of these

15. Marina used 4/9 of her money to buy 9 identical blouses and 5 identical pairs of pants. She used 1/3 of the remaining amount of money to buy another 10 identical blouses. She had ₹ 330 left. How much money did she have at first?

(a) ₹ 891 (b) ₹ 300
(c) ₹ 405 (d) None of these

16.

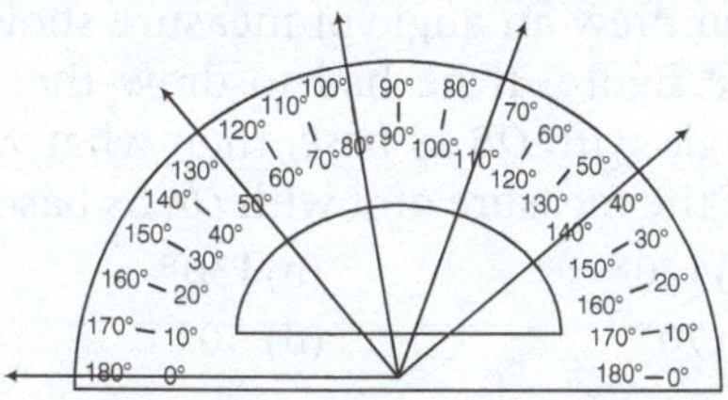

Which of the following options will have the result equal to the HCF of the above marked angles?

(a) LCM (2°, 5°) (b) HCF (10°, 100°)
(c) Both (a) and (b) (d) None of these

17. From the given diagram, what is the value of $p + q + r$?

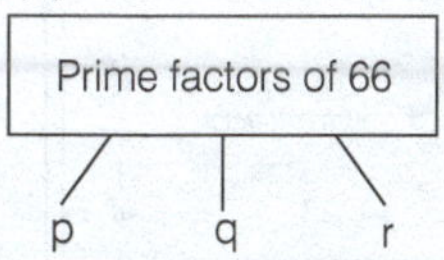

(a) 7 (b) 14 (c) 16 (d) 18

18. Match the following columns and choose the correct option.

Column A	Column B
I. Numbers which are not multiples of 2.	(i) Odd numbers
II. Numbers which have more than two factors.	(ii) Prime numbers
III. Successor of every odd number.	(iii) Composite numbers
IV. Numbers having only two factors, 1 and itself.	(iv) Even numbers

	I	II	III	IV
(a)	(i)	(ii)	(iii)	(iv)
(b)	(iv)	(iii)	(ii)	(i)
(c)	(ii)	(i)	(iii)	(iv)
(d)	(i)	(iii)	(iv)	(ii)

19. Jessica and Denmark each shaded some parts of two squares of the same size as given below.

Andrew, their friend, also shaded some parts of a square of the same size where he shaded a greater area than Jessica but a smaller area than Denmark. Which of the following can be Andrew's square?

(a)  (b) 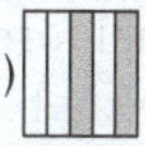

(c)  (d) 

20. Shivani works 15 h a week (Monday to Friday). Last week she worked $3\frac{1}{2}$ h on Monday, 4 h on Tuesday, $2\frac{1}{6}$ h on Wednesday and $1\frac{1}{2}$ h on Thursday. How many hours did she work on Friday?

(a) 4 h (b) $\frac{5}{6}$ h
(c) $3\frac{5}{6}$ h (d) $2\frac{5}{6}$ h

21. ITSC Bank provide the following list of value of other currency in Indian rupees :

Country	Currency	Value (in ₹)
Sri Lanka	Rupee (SL)	0.37
USA	Dollar	60.23
UAE	Dirham	11.40
England	Pound	93.75
Hong Kong	Dollar (HK)	6.20
China	Yuan	6.75

Brian living in England gets a pocket money of 15 pounds. He transferred ₹ 375.50 to his Indian friend to buy an Indian painting for himself. How much money (in Indian rupees) is left with Brian now?

(a) ₹ 900.25 (b) ₹ 1681.25
(c) ₹ 1771.75 (d) ₹ 1030.75

22. Harry distributed 236 kg of wheat into 16 people equally, then the quantity of wheat each people will get

(a) 25.63 kg (b) 16.75 kg
(c) 17.85 kg (d) 14.75 kg

23. A cyclist takes 4 h to cover the distance 95 km. Represent the speed of the cyclist into decimal form.

(a) 20 km/h (b) 23.75 km/h
(c) 41.25 km/h (d) 95 km/h

24. Every teacher is assigned with a school locker to keep their books and notebooks. If the volume of one book is 24 cubic inch, then the number of such books can be placed in the locker is

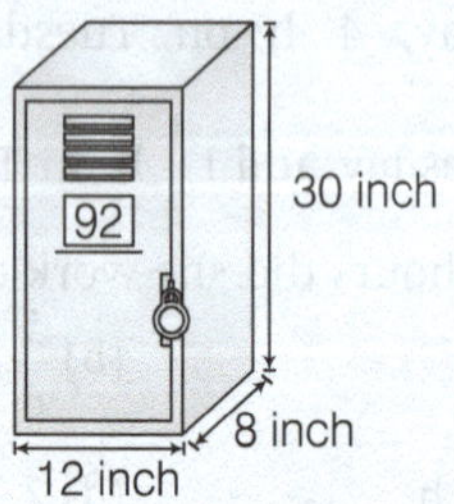

(a) 100 (b) 120
(c) 150 (d) 160

25. A big cube shaped brick of gold is melted to make small cuboid shaped biscuits of measure 30 cm × 20 cm × 0.05 m. If the edge of the brick measures 1.2 m, then the number of such biscuits can be formed is

(a) 600 (b) 696
(c) 472 (d) None of these

26.

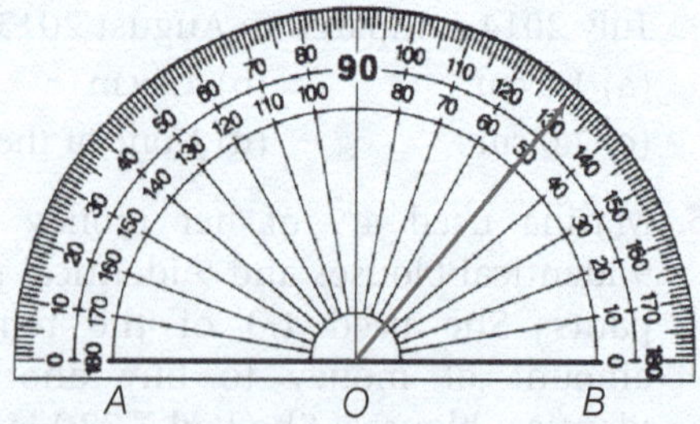

Martin's protractor got ruined and the impression of some numbers got faded. He had to draw an angle by taking *OB* as base but mistakenly he took *OA* as base and drew an angle of measure shown in the figure. If he had to draw the same angle with *OB* as base, then what would be the measure of it with *OA* as base?

(a) 120° (b) 130°
(c) 70° (d) 50°

27. Bandy needs to make rectangular invitation cards for her birthday party. She has to cut a square sheet of poster board measuring 12 inch on each side. What is the greatest number of cards that Bandy can make?

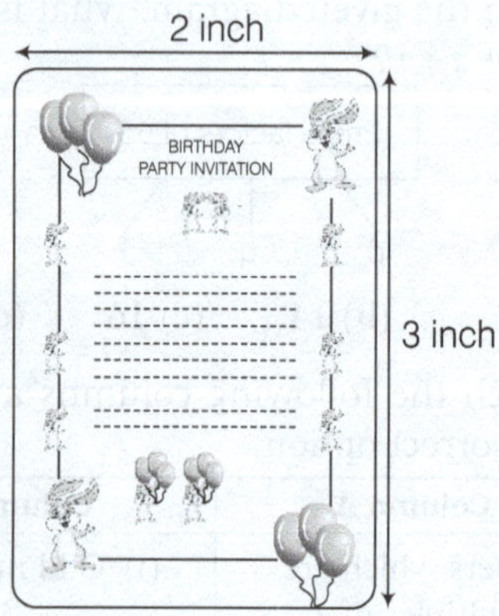

(a) 14
(b) 16
(c) 18
(d) 24

28. Luis likes to collect different types of stamps and paste it on a scrapbook of page size 7.5 cm by 6 cm. If all the stamps in a scrapbook are of same size as 2.5 cm by 1.5 cm.

How many such stamps can be collected by placing them side by side in a scrap a book having 10 such pages?

(a) 100 (b) 110
(c) 125 (d) 120

29. The cube shown below was cut into three pieces.

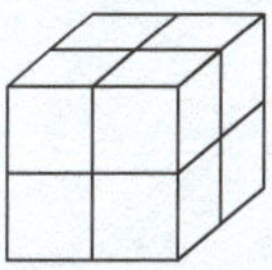

Which of the following groups can be joined to make the given cube?

(a) 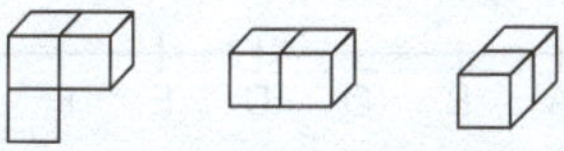

(b) 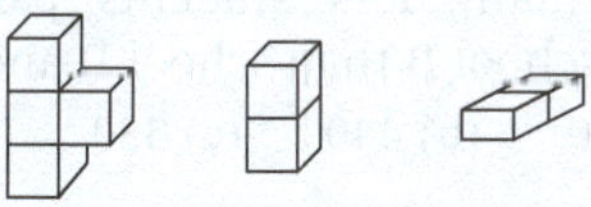

(c) 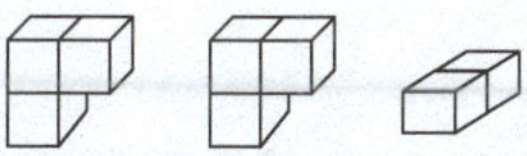

(d) None of the above

30. Find the number which is 7556456 less than the product of 9787 and 6879.

(a) 59768317
(b) 58768317
(c) 67324773
(d) 59767317

31. Which one of the following sets contains all the prime number between 1 to 30?

(a) {1, 2, 3, 5, 7, 11, 13, 19, 23, 29}
(b) {2, 3, 5, 7, 11, 13, 23, 29}
(c) {2, 3, 5, 7, 11, 13, 17, 19, 23, 29}
(d) {1, 2, 3, 5, 11, 13, 17, 19, 29}

32. X is a fraction. When X is subtracted from $\frac{3}{5}$, to get the result $\frac{7}{15}$. Find the value of X.

(a) $\frac{4}{15}$ (b) $\frac{11}{15}$
(c) $\frac{2}{15}$ (d) $\frac{1}{15}$

33. Which one of the following is the correct expanded form for the decimal 70.0302 ?

(a) $70 + \frac{3}{10} + \frac{2}{100}$
(b) $70 + \frac{3}{100} + \frac{2}{10000}$
(c) $70 + \frac{3}{100} + \frac{2}{1000}$
(d) $70 + \frac{3}{10} + \frac{2}{1000}$

34. What is the value of successor of the largest 7 digit number?

(a) 1000000
(b) 10000000
(c) 9999998
(d) None of the above

35. Jaspreet joined cooking classes on 18th March 2019 and completed on 30th June 2019. What was the duration of the classes?

(a) 102 days (b) 103 days
(c) 104 days (d) 105 days

36. The total weight of 4 people is 406 kg. In 2 of them have equal weight of 83 kg and the 3rd one weight of 79 kg. The weight of the 4th person is

(a) 109 kg (b) 161 kg
(c) 143 kg (d) 159 kg

37. Find the area of the floor whose perimeter is 74 m and length is 25 m.

(a) 250 m^2 (b) 128 m^2
(c) 300 m^2 (d) 310 m^2

38. The radius of a circle is 6.3 cm, find the circumference of the circle. (Take $\pi = \frac{22}{7}$)

(a) 39.6 cm
(b) 44 cm
(c) 12.6 cm
(d) 138.6 cm

39. Sohan knits 848 stitches. If there are 32 stitches in each row of knitting, then how many complete rows have been knitted?

(a) 26 (b) 28
(c) 29 (d) 25

40. The line graph shows the number of students participated in sports of 7 different schools. Study the graph carefully and answer the following question :

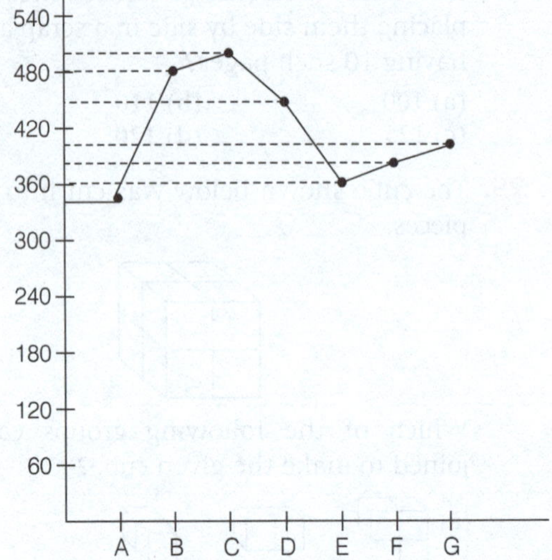

How many less students participated from school B than school D and G?

(a) 420 (b) 440 (c) 380 (d) 360

2 Marks Questions

41. The given table shows the timings of a showroom. Study it carefully and answer the question that follows.

Day	Time
Mon-Fri	9:30 am - 5:00 pm
Sat-Sun	9:45 am - 2:00 pm

Sameer arrived at the showrooom at 8:15 am on Wednesday. How long will he have to wait for the showroom to open? If he arrived at the same time on Sunday, then how long will he have to wait?

(a) 1 h 15 min, 1 h 40 min
(b) 1 h 5 min, 1 h 40 min
(c) 1 h 5 min, 1 h 30 min
(d) 1 h 15 min, 1 h 30 min

42. Write in ascending order of the following roman numbers.

XX, LIV, LXVI, LIX, XCVII, LXXXVIII

(a) XX > LIV < LIX < LXVI > LXXXVIII < XCVII
(b) XX < LIV < LIX < LXVI < LXXXVIII < XCVII
(c) XV < XX > LIV < LIX < IXIV < LXXVII
(d) None of the above

43. Select the incorrect match.

(a) Forty six lakh five hundred → 4600500

(b) Fifty lakh nine hundred three → 5009003

(c) 82464 when rounded off to nearest tens gives → 82470

(d) Predecessor of 999999 → 999998

44. If □ × □ = 36; ○ ÷ □ = 8 and ✡ + ○ = 50, then find the value of □ + ○ + ✡.

(a) 50 (b) 52

(c) 48 (d) 56

45. In 16763.632, the sum of place values of 6's and is ...... more than the sum of place values of 3.

(a) 6047.47

(b) 6067.67

(c) 6057.57

(d) 6037.37

46. Kishan spend $\frac{1}{3}$ of his salary and saved ₹ 1700 every month. How much did he earn in a year?

(a) ₹ 12600

(b) ₹ 20600

(c) ₹ 30600

(d) None of the above

47. Study the given figure and select the correct option.

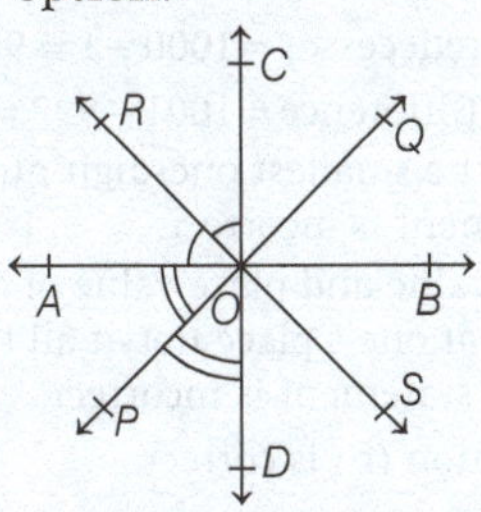

(a) ∠AOR - Acute angle

(b) ∠POR - Obtuse angle

(c) ∠AOQ - Straight angle

(d) ∠DOB - Acute angle

48. Find the area of the given figure.

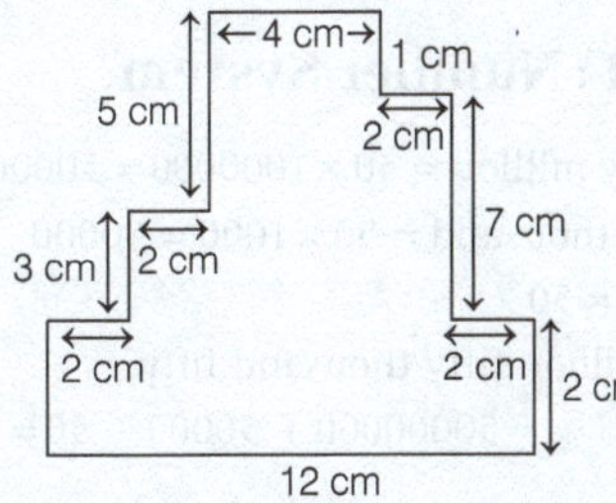

(a) 72 cm² (b) 76 cm²

(c) 96 cm² (d) 106 cm²

49. Match the figures in column I with their number of lines of symmetry in column II.

	Column I		Column II
p.		x.	3
q.		y.	1
r.	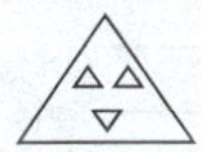	z.	2

(a) p - z, q - x, r - y (b) p - y, q - z, r - x

(c) p - x, q - y, r - z (d) None of these

50. The given bar graph shows the number of visitors who visit 5 different picnic places.

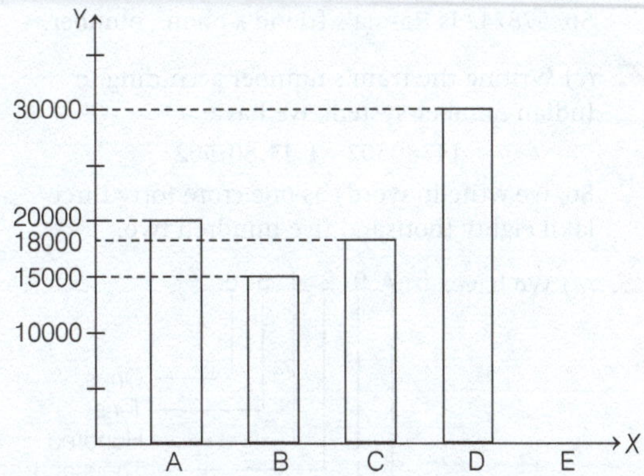

If the number of visitors of place *E* was 5000 more than the number of visitors of place *C*, then find the total number of visitors.

(a) 230000 (b) 180000

(c) 106000 (d) 96000

HINTS AND SOLUTIONS

Chapter 1 : Number System

1. *(d)* Fifty million $= 50 \times 1000000 = 50000000$

Fifty thousand $= 50 \times 1000 = 50000$

Fifty $= 50$

Fifty million fifty thousand fifty

$= 50000000 + 50000 + 50 = 50050050$

2. *(a)* As we know, one period of international system consists of 3 digits.

Since, the number, used to represent the area of Maharashtra is of the form million, hundred thousand, ten thousand, thousand, hundred, tens, ones which is an international number system.

Hence, international system is used in the numeration of the area of Maharashtra.

3. *(c)* Here, is only Option (c),

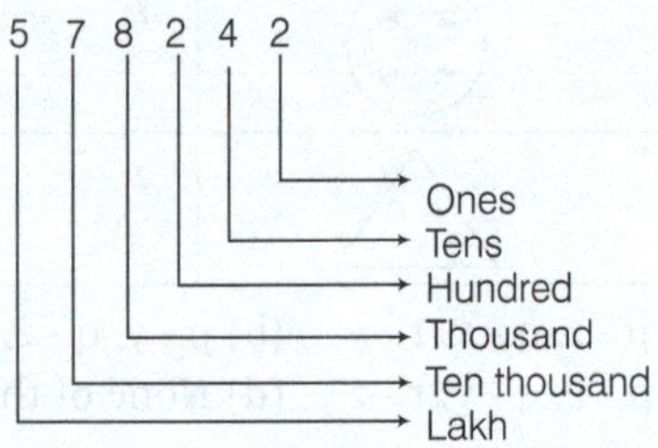

8 is on the thousand's place and 4 is on the ten's place.

So, 578242 is Ramia's friend's phone number.

4. *(c)* Writing the train's number according to Indian number system, we have

$14380502 = 1,43,80,502$

So, we write in words as one crore forty three lakh eighty thousand five hundred two.

5. *(a)* We have,

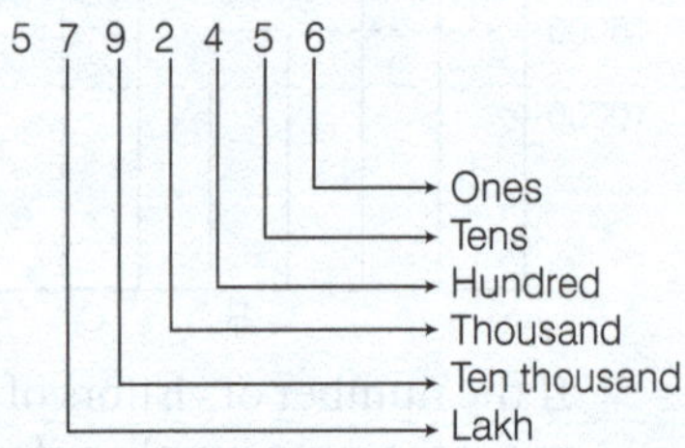

We know that 1 lakh $= 100000$

$= 1$ hundred thousand

So, the place value of 7 in 5792456 is

7 lakh $= 700000 = 7$ hundred thousand

6. *(c)* Writing the number according to Indian number system, we have

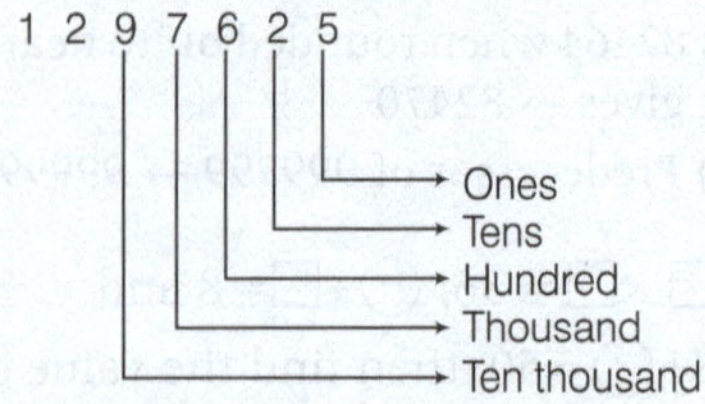

$\therefore$ Place value of $9 = 9 \times 10000$

$= 90000$ (= 90 thousand)

and face value of $9 = 9$

$\therefore$ Difference between them $= 90000 - 9 = 89991$

7. *(b)* Place value of 1 in 100000000 is 10 crore.

[as $100000000 = 10 \times 10000000 = 10$ crore]

So, the required number to be added to 3543467 to get 10 crore

$= 100000000 - \underline{3}\,\underline{5}\,\underline{4}\,\underline{3}\,\underline{4}\,\underline{6}\,\underline{7} = \underline{9}\,\underline{6}\,\underline{4}\,\underline{5}\,\underline{6}\,\underline{5}\,\underline{3}\,\underline{3}$

8. *(c)*

I. True, place value and face value are always equal for '0'.

II. False, successor of a number is one greater than the number.

III. False, place value of a digit becomes 100 times as it moves from ten's place to thousand's place.

IV. True.

9. *(b)* The statements are as follow:

(a) 99999999 is the predecessor of 100000000, so given statement is incorrect.

(b) Let 1000 be the number.

Successor $= 1000 + 1 = 1001$

and predecessor $= 1000 - 1 = 999$

$\therefore$ Difference $= 1001 - 999 = 2$, correct

(c) '1' is the smallest one-digit number, so given statement is incorrect.

(d) Face value and place value of a number are same at one's place not at all the places, so given statement is incorrect.

Hence, option (b) is correct.

10. *(a)* The correct expanded form of the area of Jim Corbett National Park is

$1217403 = 1000000 + 200000 + 10000 + 7000 + 400 + 3$

$= 1200000 + 17000 + 400 + 3$

$= 12 \times 100000 + 17 \times 1000 + 4 \times 100 + 3 \times 1$
= 12 lakh 17 thousand 4 hundred 3 ones

11. (*c*) We have the correct expansion of
$800915018 = 800000000 + 900000 + 10000 + 5000 + \underline{10} + 8$
So, the missing number is 10.

12. (*a*) We have, $19 \text{ lakh} = 19 \times 100000 = 1900000$

$$19 \text{ thousand} = 19 \times 1000 = 19000$$
$$19 \text{ hundred} = 19 \times 100 = 1900$$
$$19 = 19 \times 1 = 19$$

So, the correct expanded form of the number is
$1900000 + 19000 + 1900 + 19 = 1920919$

13. (*b*) Number of students enrolled in various schools = 5261989
Primary school students = 1965233
High school students = 2006756
$\therefore$ Middle school students
$= 5261989 - (1965233 + 2006756) = 1290000$
Number rounded off to nearest lakh = 1300000

14. (*d*) Rounding off each number of visitor to nearest thousand, we get
Alligator point = 13000 [*as* 982 > 500]
Port bella = 12000 [*as* 173 < 500]
St. Joe's island = 14000 [*as* 704 > 500]
Tucker's sound = 12000 [*as* 499 < 500]
So, the beach having number of visitors equal to 13000 estimated to nearest thousand is Alligator point.

15. (*d*)

FBD's Olympiad	Number of Students with System of Numeration						
	Ten Lakh	Lakh	Ten Thousand	Thousand	Hundred	Ten	One
Science	5	7	4	8	1	2	9
Maths	6	2	7	5	4	9	2
English	6	2	7	5	5	0	1

Here, none of these have digit 5 in lakh place.
So, option (d) is correct answer.

16. (*b*) Number of students who participated in National FBD English Olympiad = 6275501
Rounding off to nearest ten thousand, we get
6280000 [as 75501 > 75000]

17. (*b*) Rounding up 2803 gives 3000.
[*as* 3000 > 2803]
Rounding up 3745 gives 4000. [as 4000 > 3745]
So, the estimated value will be more than the actual value of papers.

18. (*a*) Given product $= 6842 \times 59$
Since 6842 rounded off to nearest hundred is 6800 and 59 rounded off to nearest ten is 60.
$\therefore$ Best estimate of product is $6800 \times 60 = 408000$

19. (*d*) Given, digits are 7,4,0,5
Number of digits required in the number = 7
Greatest number among the given digits = 7
The greatest number formed by using 4, 0 and 5 is 540. Also, it is even.
Now, 7 is the greatest among the given digits, so it will be repeated four times to form the required 7-digit number.
$\therefore$ The required number = 7777540

20. (*c*)

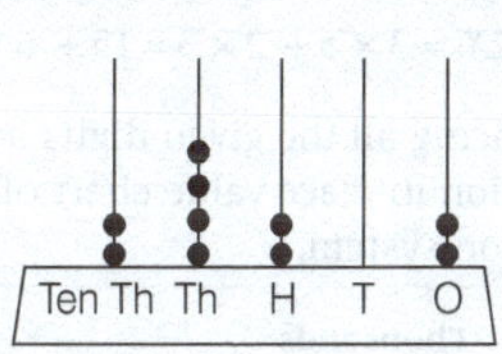

The number represented by abacus = 24202
Now, to form a number that lies between 24631 and 25212 a ring in the thousand string must be added, i.e. 1000 must be added to 24202, we get
$$24202 + 1000 = 25202$$
[*as* 24631 < 25202 < 25212]

21. (*b*) Ticket number of the students are as follow:
Amaira = 392704
Samantha = 396491
Barbara = 392677
Celia = 396449
By arranging the ticket number in ascending order, we get
$392677 < 392704 < 396449 < 396491$
So, 396491 is the largest number
Hence, Samantha has the ticket with the largest number.

22. (*b*) I. 99999 < 100000
II. 9909409 < 9990409
III. 30100100 > 30100099
So, the correct sequence is <, <, >.

23. *(c)* On solving,

$673 \times 3719 - 473 = 2502887 - 473 = 2502414$

Successor of $2502414 = 2502414 + 1 = 2502415$

On comparing, $2502XY5$, we get

$$X = 4, Y = 1$$

Predecessor of $2502414 = 2502414 - 1 = 2502413$

On comparing $P5\ Q2413$, we get

$$P = 2, Q = 0$$

So, $XY + PQ = 4 \times 1 + 2 \times 0 = 4 + 0 = 4$

24. *(d)* Place value of 'X' = $X000$

(as it is on thousand place)

Place value of 'Y' = $Y0000$

(as it is on ten thousand place)

On adding $Y0000 + X000 = Y0000$

$$\begin{array}{r} + X000 \\ \hline YX000 \end{array}$$

Comparing $YX000$ and 53000, we get

$$Y = 5, X = 3$$

So, $3Y + 2X = 3 \times 5 + 2 \times 3 = 15 + 6 = 21$

25. *(b)* By placing all the given digits according to the question in place value chart of international numeration system,

Place	Thousands			Ones		
	Hundred Thousand	Ten Thousand	Thousand	Hundred	Tens	One
	100,000	10,000	1000	100	10	1
Digits	6	9	4	1	8	0

∴ Diwakar's user ID number

$= 6 \times 100{,}000 + 9 \times 10{,}000 + 4 \times 1{,}000 + 1 \times 100 + 8 \times 10 + 0 \times 1$

$= 694180$

26. *(d)* According to the question,

Ones place > Hundreds place digit > Thousands place digit.

In the given option, only option (d) satisfies the above condition.

$\because \quad 7 > 5 > 4$

∴ Required Answer = 574,567

27. *(a)* We know that the even prime number is 2.

∴ Unit place digit of number = 2

The smallest prime odd number is 3.

∴ The hundred's place digit = 3

The smallest odd number is 1.

∴ The thousand's place digit = 1

From all options other 2 digits of number are 6 and 5.

Here 5 is the predecessor of 6.

∴ Ten place digits = 5

and ten thousand's place digit = 6

∴ Required number = 61352

Chapter 2 : Roman Numerals

1. *(c)* We know,

$495 = (500 - 100) + (100 - 10) + 5 = $ CD X CV

∴ Middle letter should be interchanged by the next letter.

2. *(d)* We know,

$999 = (1000 - 100) + (100 - 10) + (10 - 1)$

$=$ CMXCIX

∴ C should be place left to the I.

3. *(b)* Now LXV − IX = $(50 + 10 + 5) - (9)$

$= 65 - 9 = 56 = $ LVI

4. *(d)* We know, CM = $(1000 - 100) = 900$

If symbols place interchanged, then we get

MC = $1000 + 100 = 1100$

∴ Increase in the number $= 1100 - 900 = 200$

5. *(d)* As we know, 1 matchstick = 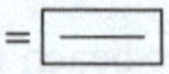 (given)

So, X is made from 2 matchsticks and also L is made from 2 matchsticks, therefore 40 = XL = Made up of 4 matchsticks.

6. *(b)* We know, XLV = $(50 - 10) + 5 = 45$

and III = 3

∴ XLV ÷ III = $45 \div 3 = 15 = 10 + 5 = $ XV

7. *(b)* We know, L = 50

$\bar{\text{L}} = 50 \times 1000 = 50000$; D = 500

If the value of $\bar{\text{L}}$ will be n times of D, then

$$\bar{\text{L}} = n \times \text{D} \Rightarrow n = \frac{\bar{\text{L}}}{\text{D}} = \frac{50 \times 1000}{500} = 100$$

So, the resultant value becomes 100 times of the value of D.

8. *(a)* Using digit 0, 2, 8 only once,

Greatest 3-digit number = 820

We can write,

820 = 500 + 100 + 100 + 100 + 10 + 10 = DCCCXX

9. (c) We know that,

DCLX = 500 + 100 + 50 + 10 = 660,
CDCX = (500 – 100) + (100 + 10) = 510,
CDXL = (500 – 100) + (50 – 10) = 440,
and DCXL = 500 + 100 + (50 – 10) = 640

∵ 440 is the least value in 660, 510, 440 and 640.

∴ CDXL is least in the given options.

10. (a) We Know that,

XXI = 21, XV = 15, LIX = 59
LXI = 61, XXIX = 29 and XCIX = 99

∵ 15 < 21 < 29 < 59 < 61 < 99

∴ XV < XXI < XXIX < LIX < LXI < XCIX

11. (d) We know that, $\overline{\text{X}} = 10 \times 1000 = 10000$,

D = 500, C = 100, $X = 10$, V = 5 and I = 1

$10638 = 10000 + 500 + 100 + 10 + 10 + 10 + 5 + 1 + 1 + 1$

$= \overline{\text{X}} + \text{D} + \text{C} + \text{X} + \text{X} + \text{X} + \text{V} + \text{I} + \text{I} + \text{I}$

$= \overline{\text{X}}\text{DCXXXVIII}$

12. (c) We already know that 3 digit greatest number = 999

and 3 digit smallest number = 100

∴ $K = 999 - 100 = 899$

∵ The roman numeral for (K = 899)

= 500 + 100 + 100 + 100 + (100 – 10) + (10 – 1)
= DCCCXCIX

13. (c) We have neither L nor D, so we can not form any number with the help of 50 or 500.

So, we cannot form/write 1947, 1548 and 1753 by using the given roman numerals.

∴ 1118 = 1000 + 100 + 10 + 5 + 1 + 1 + 1 = MCXVIII

∴ 1118 can be written.

14. (b) Now, (A) LXXXVIII

= L + XXX + V + III = 50 + 30 + 5 + 3 = 88

(B) XCVIII = XC + V + III = 90 + 5 + 3 = 98,

(C) LXIX = L + X + IX = 50 + 10 + 9 = 69,

(D) CLX = C + L + X = 100 + 50 + 10 = 160,

(E) XXXIX = XXX + IX = 30 + 9 = 39.

15. (b) From roman numerals, DCCCVI

= 500 + 100 + 100 + 100 + 5 + 1 = 806

CCMVI = 100 + (1000 – 100) + 5 + 1

= 1000 + 6 = 10006

Here, DCCCVI > CCMVI

Chapter 3 : Operations on Numbers

1. (d) We have,

```
    1 1 1 ←Carry
  8 4 3 6 7 1
+     5 3 2 9
  -----------
  8 4 9 0 0 0
```

In fourth column, we will 5, 3 and carry 1 so the sum will be 9, not 8.

∴ There is a mistake in fourth column from right.

2. (a) Number shown on abacus = 151203

∴ Number, which is 2631 more than the abacus's number = 151203 + 2631 = 153834

3. (b) From the given numbers, we find that

From option (a), 479 – 277 = 202
From option (b), 582 – 277 = 305
From option (c), 582 – 316 = 266
From option (d), 479 – 316 = 163

Hence, option (b) is correct.

4. (a) Given that, $A + B = C - B$

which means $A + B + B = C$

⇒ $76240 + 3245 + 3245 = C$

∴ $C = 82730$

5. (d) Total number of people in the city = 100000

Number of people of age below 20 = 34768

Number of people of age between 20 and 30 = 57498

So, number of people of age above 30

= Remaining people of city
= 100000 – (34768 + 57498)
= 100000 – 92266 = 7734

6. (d) From the given number line, the difference between every two consecutive markings is 10.

So, $X = 3960$ and $Y = 4800$

∴ Required difference = $Y - X$ = 4800 – 3960 = 40

7. (b) Using digits 8, 5, 9, 1, 2 and 3 only once, make 6 digit greatest number = 985321

[∵ by arranging the given digits in descending order]

6 digit least number = 123589

[∵ by arranging the given digits in ascending order]

$\therefore$ Their difference $= 985321$
$\quad -123589$
$\quad 861732$

8. *(c)* Given, $\triangle + \triangle + \square = 255$

and $\triangle - \square = 30$

$\Rightarrow \quad 3\triangle = 255 + 30 = 285$

$\therefore \quad \triangle = 95$

9. *(c)* Given, cost of one cupcake is ₹ 10.

$\therefore$ Cost of four cupcakes $= 4 \times 10 =$ ₹ 40

So, multiplying 4 with the price (or multiplying 10 by 4) will give the answer.

10. *(a)* Since, $123456 = ABCDE \times 4$

So, $\quad ABCDE = 123456 \div 4 = 30864$

Hence, option (a) is the correct answer.

11. *(d)* Distance of the car route = 9 km

Distance covered by car in a day

$= 2 \times 9 = 18$ km

Now, distance covered by car in 5 days

$= 18 \times 5 = 90$ km

12. *(c)* Option (a), $45789 \times 1 = 45789$

Option (b), $4579 \times 0 = 0$

Option (c), $45789 \times 10 = 457890$

Option (d), $45789 - 0 = 45789$

Hence, option (c) is incorrect.

13. *(c)* Number of adult tickets = 467

Cost of 1 adult ticket = ₹ 9

$\therefore$ Total cost of adult tickets $= 467 \times 9$

Number of youth tickets = 215

Cost of 1 youth ticket = ₹ 4

So, total cost of youth tickets $= 215 \times 4$

$\therefore$ Difference between the cost of adult tickets and youth tickets $= (467 \times 9) - (215 \times 4)$

14. *(b)* The missing numbers are as follow :

(i) $\rightarrow 50 \times 10 = 500$ (ii) $\rightarrow 6 \times 7 = 42$

(iii) $\rightarrow 500 + 350 = 850$ (iv) $\rightarrow 60 + 42 = 102$

15. *(b)* Total number of sweets distributed = 2961

Number of sweets each child received = 3

So, total number of children $= 2961 \div 3 = 987$

16. *(a)* Number of rows of mango trees = 15

Number of mango trees in each row = 325

So, total number of mango trees $= 325 \times 15 = 4875$

Number of rows cut down = 6

So, number of mango trees cut down

$= 6 \times 325 = 1950$

Therefore, total number of mango trees left

$= 4875 - 1950 = 2925$

17. *(a)*

I. False, only 1 divisible by 1 gives quotient equal to 1.

II. True, e.g. $\frac{100}{10} = 10, \frac{1020}{10} = 102$

III. True, LHS $= (4 \times 6) + (4 \times 10) = 24 + 40 = 64$

RHS $= 4 \times (6 + 10) = 4 \times 16 = 64$

So, LHS = RHS

IV. True (by definition)

18. *(c)* According to the rule of operations (or DMAS), division is used first.

$\therefore \quad 7 + 21 \div 3 - 8 \times 2 + 9$

$= 7 + 7 - 8 \times 2 + 9$

So, the first step is $21 \div 3$.

Therefore, Sanchi did the correct step.

19. *(c)* We have, start number $\div 45 \times 24 = 720$

So, the start number $= 720 \times 45 \div 24$

$= \frac{720 \times 45}{24} = 30 \times 45 = 1350$

20. *(b)* Given, $A + A + A + A + A + A + A + A + A + A + A = 25465099$

On adding, $11A = 25465099$

$\Rightarrow \quad A = \frac{25465099}{11}$

By long division method,

11)25465099(2315009
−22
34
− 33
16
−11
55
−55
99
−99
×

$\therefore \quad A = 2315009$

and $\quad 4A = 2315009 \times 4$

$= 9260036$

21. *(a)* Here, collection made by each class is as follows :

Class 1 = $728 \times 25 = 18200$

Class 2 = $225 \times 40 = 9000$

Class 3 = $374 \times 20 = 7480$

and Class 4 = $280 \times 30 = 8400$

Here, 18200 is the greatest number.

So, class 1 collected the maximum number of food items.

22. *(c)* Number of packets collected by class 1 $= 728 \times 25 = 18200$

If class 2 has to collect 18200 packets in 40 days, then the number of packets it must collect each day $= 18200 \div 40 = 455$

23. *(d)* We know, if the product/multiplication of 695 and $52AA72A = 3645083180$

$\therefore 695 \times 52AA72A = 3645083180$

$\Rightarrow \quad 52AA72A = \dfrac{3645083180}{695}$

$\Rightarrow \quad 52AA72A = 5244724$

On comparison, $A = 4$

$\therefore$ The value of $1015 \times A = 1015 \times 4$

$= 4060$

24. *(b)* From the given table, we have

A = 4520 + 5345 = 9865

B = 4520 + 7200 = 11720

C = 9100 + 5345 = 14445

D = 9100 + 7200 = 16300

$\therefore (A + B) - (C + D)$

$= (9865 + 11720) - (14445 + 16300)$

$= 21585 - 30745 = -9160$

Chapter 4 : Factors and Multiples

1. *(c)* We have factor tree of 90 is as follows

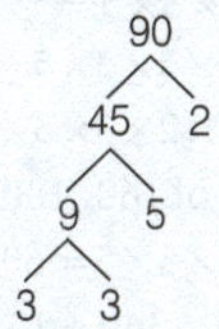

So, option (c) is correct.

2. *(b)* We have factor tree of 150 is as follows

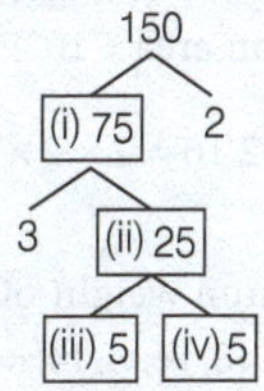

So, (i) $\rightarrow$ 75, (ii) $\rightarrow$ 25, (iii) $\rightarrow$ 5 and (iv) $\rightarrow$ 5

3. *(c)* We have ,

Multiples of 2 = 2, 4, 6, 8, 10, 12, 14, 16, 18, ...

Multiples of 4 = 4, 8, 12, 16, 20, ...

Multiples of 8 = 8, 16, 24, ...

So,

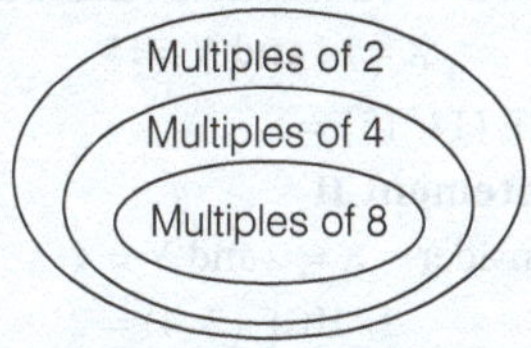

Therefore, Jimmy had drawn the correct picture.

4. *(b)* Here, HCF (22, 33) = 11

[$\because 22 = 2 \times 11$ and $33 = 3 \times 11$]

HCF (20, ?) = 5

So, the missing number is 15.

[as HCF (20, 15) = 5, where $20 = 5 \times 4$ and $15 = 5 \times 3$]

5. *(b)* Number of onions = $56 = 2 \times 2 \times 2 \times 7$

Number of potatoes = $32 = 2 \times 2 \times 2 \times 2 \times 2$

Number of tomatoes = 64

$= 2 \times 2 \times 2 \times 2 \times 2 \times 2$

The maximum number of vegetables of same type he can keep in each basket

= HCF (56, 32, 64) = $2 \times 2 \times 2 = 8$

6. *(a)* Number of onions = 56

Number of potatoes = 32

Number of tomatoes = 64

HCF (56, 32, 64) = 8

[as in the above question]

Number of baskets of onions = $\dfrac{56}{8} = 7$

Number of baskets of potatoes = $\dfrac{32}{8} = 4$

Number of baskets of tomatoes = $\dfrac{64}{8} = 8$

7. *(a)* We have, $\quad 80 = 2 \times 2 \times 2 \times 2 \times 5$

$110 = 2 \times 5 \times 11$

$\therefore$ HCF (80, 110) = 2×5

So, the common area = HCF (80, 110)= 2×5

8. *(d)* $8 = 2\times 2\times 2, 16 = 2\times 2\times 2\times 2, 4 = 2\times 2,$

$14 = 2\times 7$

So, the maximum weight of each packet

= HCF (8, 16, 4, 14) = 2 units

9. *(b)* $4 = 2\times 2,\ 5 = 5\times 1,\ 6 = 2\times 3$

The day when all the books will be read together = LCM (4, 5, 6) = $2\times 2\times 3\times 5$ = 60 th day

10. *(c)* **Statement I**

Consider, two coprime numbers

X = 14 and Y = 15

HCF (14, 15) = 1

Statement II

Consider X = 2 and Y = 4

HCF (2, 4) = 2

Also, $4 \div 2 = 2$

Hence, both statements are correct.

11. *(d)* Using prime factorisation method,

3	4845
5	1615
17	323
19	19
	1

$\therefore 4845 = 3\times 5\times 17\times 19$

$\therefore$ (3, 5) and (17, 19) are twin primes,

i.e. P and S are the required twin primes.

12. *(d)* Given one number = 10 + 2 = 12

We know that,

product of two number = HCF × LCM

One number × Other number = HCF × LCM

12 × Other number = 4 × 48

$\therefore$ Other number = $\frac{4\times 48}{12} = 16$

13. *(a)* Annie's score → lowest multiple of 10 = 10

Jass's score → fourth multiple of 3 = 12 (i.e., 3×4)

Krish's score → highest factor of 15 = 15

By arranging the scores in ascending order, we get 15 < 12 < 10

So, Annie < Jass < Krish.

14. *(b)* Margret went for singing class on every 3rd day, dancing class on every 4th day and drawing class on every 6th day.

The day on which she will go for all her classes

= LCM (3, 4, 6) = 12th

The day on which she went for all the three classes before = 5th, Monday

So, the next time she will go for all the three classes on the same day = 5 + 12

= 17th, Saturday

15. *(c)* $40 = 2\times 2\times 2\times 5, 60 = 2\times 2\times 3\times 5$

$50 = 2\times 5\times 5$

The time when water in all the colours will be erected out from the fountain

= LCM (40, 50, 60)

= $2\times 2\times 2\times 3\times 5\times 5 = 600$

= 600 min = 10 h

So, after 8 am the water in all colours will be erected at 6 pm.

16. *(c)* LCM of above two numbers = HCF of below two numbers, i.e. LCM (2, 3) = 6

HCF (12, 30) = 6

Now, HCF of (36, 60) = 12

LCM of (4, x) = 12 = $2\times 2\times 3$

So, from the given options, $x = 6$

17. *(c)* Using prime factorisation method to find LCM and HCF of M and N respectively.

2	18, 24, 40
2	9, 12, 20
2	9, 6, 10
3	9, 3, 5
3	3, 1, 5
5	1, 1, 5
	1, 1, 1

M = LCM of (18, 24, 40)

= $2\times 2\times 2\times 3\times 3\times 5 = 360$

Now, $60 = 2\times 2\times 3\times 5$

$180 = 2\times 2\times 3\times 3\times 5$

$360 = 2\times 2\times 2\times 3\times 3\times 5$

N = HCF of (60, 180, 360)

= $2\times 2\times 3\times 5 = 60$

$\therefore\ 5M + 15N = 5\times 360 + 15\times 60$

= 1800 + 900 = 2700

$\therefore$ Digit is on the thousand place of the number = 2

18. *(b)* I. Given, HCF of numbers = 2

and LCM of numbers = 60

So, product of numbers = $60 \times 2 = 120$

and $120 = (2 \times 60), (3 \times 40), (4 \times 30), (5 \times 24),$

$(6 \times 20), (8 \times 15), (10 \times 12)$

Also, HCF of numbers = 3

and LCM of numbers = 90

$\therefore$ Product of numbers = $3 \times 90 = 270$

and $270 = (2 \times 135), (3 \times 90), (5 \times 54), (6 \times 45),$

$(9 \times 30), (10 \times 27), (15 \times 18)$

So, there are more than three such pairs.

Hence, Luke is correct.

Chapter 5 : Fractions

1. *(c)* Number of vowels = 5 (a, e, i, o, u)

Number of Consonants = 21

Fraction of vowels to consonants = $\frac{5}{21}$

2. *(a)* We have the simplest form as

$\frac{3}{15} = \frac{1}{5}, \frac{16}{31} = \frac{16}{31}, \frac{9}{17} = \frac{9}{17}$ and $\frac{4}{5} = \frac{4}{5}$

So, $\frac{3}{15}$ is incorrect as it is not in the correct simplest form while all others are in the simplest form.

3. *(c)* Part of the class assignment coloured by

Yamini $= 1 + 1 + 1 + 1 + \frac{3}{7} = 4 + \frac{3}{7}$

$= \frac{28 + 3}{7} = \frac{31}{7} = 4\frac{3}{7}$

So, marks obtained by Yamini = $4\frac{3}{7}$

4. *(b)* Total number of shapes = $6 \times 4 = 24$

Number of stars drawn = 8

$\therefore$ The part of picture which are having stars

$= \frac{8}{24} = \frac{1}{3}$

5. *(b)* Number of shaded parts = 9

Total number of parts = 13

Here, two more parts can be drawn.

So, total number of parts in the figure

$= 13 + 2 = 15$

Now, $\frac{2}{3} \times$ Total parts $= \frac{2}{3} \times 15 = 10$

So, the more number of shaded parts should be

$= 10 - 9 = 1$

Remaining parts (not to be shaded) = $2 - 1 = 1$

$\therefore$ Number of unshaded part to be added = 1

6. *(c)* Here, $1\frac{9}{10} = 1 + \frac{9}{10} = \frac{19}{10}$

Now, $\frac{10}{10} < \frac{19}{10} < \frac{20}{10}$ i.e. $1 < \frac{19}{10} < 2$

Dividing the part on scale between 1 and 2 in 10 equal parts

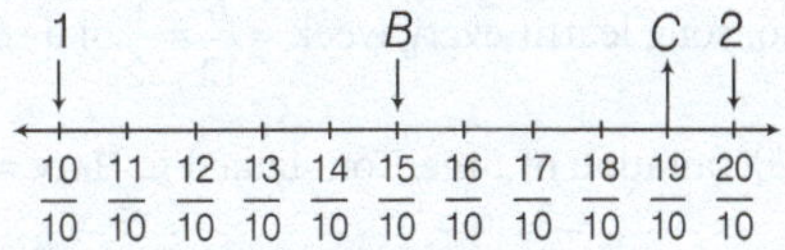

So, point C represents $\frac{19}{10} = 1\frac{9}{10}$.

7. *(d)* Number of triangles that having holes = 9

Number of triangles that having odd number of holes = 6

So, the required fraction = $\frac{6}{9} = \frac{2}{3}$

8. *(b)* Total number of square boxes = 16

I. Number of boxes coloured red = 4

$\therefore$ Fraction of boxes coloured red = $\frac{4}{16} = \frac{1}{4}$

II. Number of boxes coloured green $= 1 + \frac{1}{2} + \frac{1}{2}$

$= 2$

So, fraction of boxes which are coloured green

$= \frac{2}{16} = \frac{1}{8}$

III. Number of boxes coloured blue = 1

So, required fraction = $\frac{1}{16}$

$\therefore$ I $\rightarrow$ (iii), II $\rightarrow$ (i), III $\rightarrow$ (ii)

Hence, option (b) is correct.

9. *(b)*

(a) Number of pies each one get = $\frac{24}{8} \neq \frac{8}{24}$

(b) Part of day when Grimmy sleeps = $\frac{8}{24} = \frac{8}{24}$

(c) Number of bananas in each shake = $\frac{2 \times 12}{8}$

$= \frac{24}{8} \neq \frac{8}{24}$

(d) Number of toys received by each group

$= \frac{24}{8} \neq \frac{8}{24}$

10. (*c*) Part of cake left for Greg's friends

$= \frac{1}{2} + \frac{1}{4} = \frac{3}{4}$

$\therefore$ Part of cake eaten by Greg $= 1 - \frac{3}{4} = \frac{1}{4}$

11. (*d*) Number of weeks of summer vacation = 12

Number of songs learnt in 12 weeks = 6

So, song learnt every week $= \frac{6}{12} = \frac{1}{2}$ of a song

12. (*b*) Duration of time, Tom talked to Hary $= \frac{1}{6}$ h

Duration of time, Tom talked to Geet $= \frac{5}{3}$ h

Duration of time, Tom talked to Ryan $= \frac{1}{4}$ h

Total time spent on the telephone by Tom

$= \frac{1}{6} + \frac{5}{3} + \frac{1}{4} = \frac{2 + 20 + 3}{12}$

[by taking LCM (6, 3, 4) = $2 \times 2 \times 3 = 12$]

$= \frac{25}{12} = 2\frac{1}{12}$ h

13. (*c*) I. True, $2 \times \frac{1}{5} = \frac{2}{1} \times \frac{1}{5} = \frac{2}{5}$

II. False, $15 \times \frac{1}{10} = \frac{15}{10} = \frac{3}{2}$

III. True, $1 + 1 + 1 + \frac{1}{2} = 3\frac{1}{2}$

IV. False,

$\frac{2}{3}, \frac{4}{6}$ and $\frac{18}{27}$ are proper fractions as numerator is smaller than denominator.

14. (*d*) I. Improper, since 16 > 13

i.e. numerator > denominator

II. $\frac{5}{4}$

III. Unlike

IV. The additive inverse of $\frac{3}{7}$ is $-\frac{3}{7}$

15 (*c*) Compare the scores obtained by each player.

$\frac{75}{100}, \frac{46}{50}, \frac{54}{60}, \frac{72}{100}, \frac{89}{100}$

Converting them to equivalent fraction by multiply the numerator and denominator by a common number.

By taking LCM and converting them into equivalent fraction, we get

$\frac{225}{300}, \frac{276}{300}, \frac{270}{300}, \frac{216}{300}, \frac{267}{300}$

[$\because$ LCM (100, 50, 60) = 300]

On arranging the numerator in descending order, we get 276 > 270 > 267 > 225 > 216

[since, denominator are equal]

Therefore, we get

Shim > Rose > Den > Ken > Jack

Hence, Shim scored the highest.

16. (*a*) Highest score (of Shim) $= \frac{46}{50}$

and lowest score (of Jack) $= \frac{72}{100}$

$\therefore$ Difference between their scores $= \frac{46}{50} - \frac{72}{100}$

$= \frac{92}{100} - \frac{72}{100} = \frac{20}{100} = \frac{1}{5}$

17. (*d*) As each slice is $\frac{1}{6}$th of the pizza.

So, number of pizza slice in one pizza = 6

Total pizzas = 4

So, total number of pizza slices $= 6 \times 4 = 24$

Number of slice each one of 8 people gets $= \frac{24}{8} = 3$

18. (*c*) Time taken by Jinny to walk to the playground $= \frac{5}{6}$ h

Time taken by Jinny to walk from the playground to school $= \frac{1}{4}$ h

So, time taken by Jinny to walk to the playground and then to school

$= \frac{5}{6} + \frac{1}{4} = \frac{10 + 3}{12} = \frac{13}{12} = 1\frac{1}{12}$ h

19. (*a*) A represents $= \frac{3}{14}$ and *B* represents $= \frac{4}{14}$

According to the question,

Fraction of distance covered by A to the distance B,

$A \div B = \frac{3}{14} \div \frac{4}{14} = \frac{3}{14} \times \frac{14}{4} = \frac{3}{4}$

20. (*a*) On combining 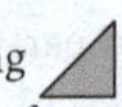 and 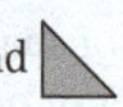 we get one shaded square.

Like combining  and , we get one shaded square.

$\therefore$ Total number of shaded squares = 7

and total number of squares = 16

$\therefore$ Required fraction $= \frac{7}{16}$.

21. *(a)* Here, shaded part in Fig. I $= 1 + \frac{10}{12}$

$$= 1 + \frac{5}{6} = 1\frac{5}{6} = \frac{11}{6}$$

and shaded part in Fig. II $= 1 + \frac{12}{20} = 1 + \frac{3}{5}$

$$= 1\frac{3}{5} = \frac{8}{5}$$

Now, on comparing $\frac{11}{6}$ and $\frac{8}{5}$, we get

$$\frac{55}{30}, \frac{48}{30}$$

[by converting them into equivalent fractions]

$\therefore \quad \frac{11}{6} > \frac{8}{5} \quad [\because 55 > 48]$

So, Shaded part of Fig. I > Shaded part of Fig. II

22. *(c)* Given expression

$$3\frac{3}{20} \times 2\frac{1}{3} + 2\frac{1}{2} - \left(5\frac{2}{7} \div \frac{1}{7}\right) = \boxed{?} \times 270\frac{3}{2}$$

Before solving the expression, change all mixed fractions into equivalent improper fraction.

$$\frac{63}{20} \times \frac{7}{3} + \frac{5}{2} - \left(\frac{37}{7} \div \frac{1}{7}\right) = \boxed{?} \times \frac{543}{2}$$

On solving,

$$\frac{21}{20} \times \frac{7}{1} + \frac{5}{2} - \left(\frac{37}{7} \times \frac{7}{1}\right) = \boxed{?} \times \frac{543}{2}$$

$$\frac{147}{20} + \frac{5}{2} - \frac{37}{1} = \boxed{?} \times \frac{543}{2}$$

$$\frac{147 + 50 - 740}{20} = \boxed{?} \times \frac{543}{2}$$

$$\therefore \quad ? = \frac{2}{20} \times \frac{-543}{543} = -\frac{1}{10}.$$

23. *(d)*

(i) There are total number of triangles 16.
Number of shaded triangles = 8
∴ The shaded fraction of the given figure

$$= \frac{8}{16} = \frac{1}{2} \quad \text{(True)}$$

(ii) Fraction of green balls $= \frac{5}{3 + 5 + 9} = \frac{5}{17}$

(iii) 21 sixth $= 21 \times \frac{1}{6} = \frac{21}{6}$ (True)

$$= 3\frac{3}{6} = 3\frac{1}{2} \neq 3\frac{1}{3} \quad \text{(False)}$$

Chapter 6 : Decimals

1. *(a)* We can put these digits in decimal place value chart,

Place	Digits
Tens (10)	
Ones (1)	90
Decimal point	.
Tenth $\left(\frac{1}{10}\right)$	3
Hundredth $\left(\frac{1}{100}\right)$	4

∴ Required decimal number

$$= (90 \times 1) + \left(3 \times \frac{1}{10}\right) + \left(4 \times \frac{1}{100}\right)$$

$$= 90 + 0.3 + 0.04 = 90.34$$

2. *(d)* To find the place value of the digit, put these digits in decimal place value chart.

Place	Digits
Tens (10)	1
Ones (1)	2
Decimal point	.
Tenth $\left(\frac{1}{10}\right)$	1
Hundredth $\left(\frac{1}{100}\right)$	4
Thousandth $\left(\frac{1}{1000}\right)$	6

∴ The place value of 4 = 4 Hundreadth

$$= 4 \times \frac{1}{100} = \frac{4}{100} = 0.04$$

3. *(c)* Fraction is changed into a decimal number by division.

$$\therefore \quad \frac{5}{10000} = 0.0005$$

Now, given addition = 700 + 40 + 0.0005

= 740.0005

4. *(b)* Given decimal = 98.25

$$= \frac{9825}{100} = \frac{393 \times 25}{4 \times 25} = \frac{393}{4}$$

5. *(c)* B is mid of 7.30 and 7.60

$\therefore$ Value of $B = \frac{7.30 + 7.60}{2} = \frac{14.90}{2} = 7.45$

The number line is as follows :

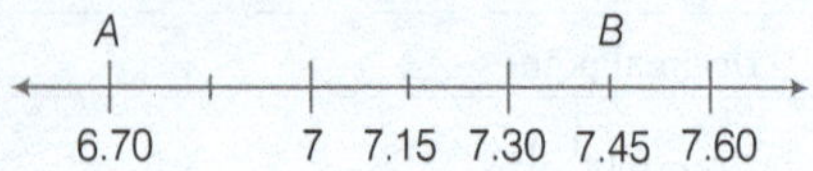

So, A = 6.70 and B = 7.45

Now, A + B = 6.70 + 7.45 = 14.15

6. *(b)* Number of squares shaded = 29

Since, each □ = 0.02

So, decimal represent by the shaded squares
$= 29 \times 0.02 = 0.58$

7. *(c)* Present height of Andrew + 35cm = 2.5m

So, present height of Andrew

$= 2.5\text{m} - 35\text{cm}$

$= 2.5\text{m} - 0.35\text{m}$ $\left[\because 1 \text{ cm} = \frac{1}{100}\text{m}\right]$

$= 2.15\text{m}$

$\therefore$ Andrew's present height = 2.15 m

8. *(a)* Given, A = 31.36 and B = 45.63

$\therefore$ 2A − B = 2 × 31.36 − 45.63

= 62.72 − 45.63 = 17.09

9. *(a)* Paint left in each paint pot is as follows :

(I) 1.2 L (II) 1.09 L

(III) 0.99 L (IV) 0.10 L

So, the total quantity of paint left

= 1.2 L + 1.09 L + 0.99 L + 0.10 L = 3.38 L

10. *(b)* Quantity of paint used from each paint pot is as follows :

I. 2 − 1.2 L = 0.8 L II. 2 − 1.09 L = 0.91 L

III. 2 − 0.99 L = 1.01 L IV. 2 − 0.10 L = 1.9 L

So, the difference between the maximum and minimum quantity of paint used

= 1.9 L − 0.8 L = 1.1 L

11. *(c)* As we know, a decimal number contains

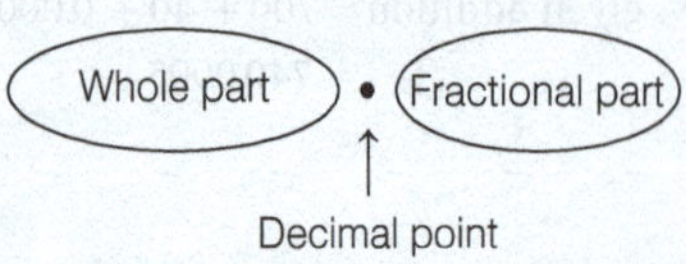

Here, whole part = 2 more than $\left(\frac{2}{5} \text{of } 20\right)$

$= \left(\frac{2}{5} \text{ of } 20\right) + 2 = \left(\frac{2}{5} \times 20\right) + 2 = 8 + 2 = 10$

and Decimal part = 3 less than $\left[\frac{1}{4} \text{of } 32\right]$

$= \left[\frac{1}{4} \text{of } 32\right] - 3 = \left(\frac{1}{4} \times 32\right) - 3$

$= 8 - 3 = 5$

$\therefore$ Decimal number = 10.5

12. *(d)*

I. The fraction $\frac{6}{25}$ is equal to decimal number <u>0.24</u>.

II. 15.8 − 6.73 = <u>9.07</u>

III. 9.07 rounded off to nearest tenth is <u>9.1</u> as 7 > 5, so 9.07 = 9.1 when rounded off to nearest tenth.

IV. 9.037 rounded off to nearest tenth is <u>9.0</u>.

13. *(c)* The complete figure is as follows :

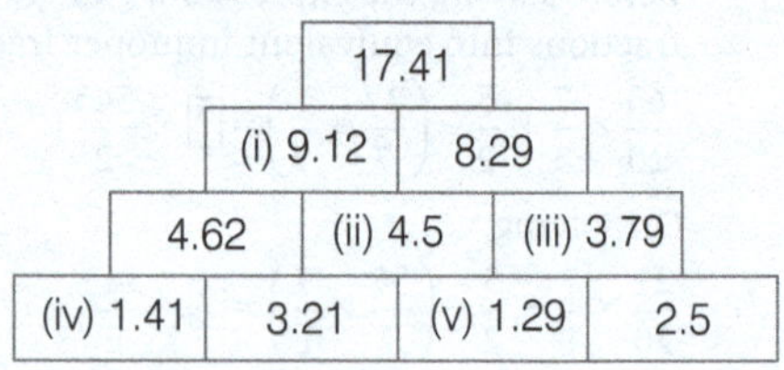

Here, (i) = 17.41 − 8.29 = 9.12

(ii) = 9.12 − 4.62 = 4.5

(iii) = 8.29 − 4.5 = 3.79

(iv) = 4.62 − 3.21 = 1.41

(v) = 4.5 − 3.21 = 1.29

14. *(a)* I. True, 15.73 = 15.7 (as 3 < 5)

II. False, 6 hundredth is written as 0.06.

III. False, digit 5 in 24.56 stands for 5 tenth.

IV. False, 0.023 lies between 0.02 and 0.03.

15. *(a)* The given numbers when rounded off to two decimal places will be equal to

4.123 ⟶ 4.12 [$\because$ 3 < 5]

7.299 ⟶ 7.30 [$\because$ 9 > 5]

14.756 ⟶ 14.76 [$\because$ 6 > 5]

0.014 ⟶ 0.01 [$\because$ 4 < 5]

16. *(a)* We have the sequence of jumps made by the five children in descending order as

4.50 > 4.28 > 4.06 > 3.99 > 3.09

So, Alex won the long jump competition.

17. (c) 11.123, 11.312, 11.415, 11.606 is the correct order of decimal numbers. Since, integral parts of these numbers are equal,
so on comparing decimal parts, we find that $123 < 312 < 415 < 606$, so they are in correct ascending order.

18. (b) Ascending order of the energy provided by each food item is

$$4.09 < 4.25 < 4.31 < 4.72$$

So, the names of the food items according to the above ascending order is

Milk < Wheat < Rice < Potatoes

19. (c) Total amount of energy provided by all food items = 4.25 J + 4.31 J + 4.72 J + 4.09 J = 17.37 J

20. (b) (a) $2A + B + C = 1834.700$

$$\begin{array}{r} 434.170 \\ 1201.234 \\ \hline 3470.104 \\ \hline \end{array}$$

which is not equal to the given decimal number.

(b) $A + 2B + C - 917.350$

$$\begin{array}{r} 868.340 \\ 1201.234 \\ \hline 2986.824 \\ \hline \end{array}$$

which is equal to the given decimal number.

21. (c) Age of youngest sister of Tyran = 9 years
∴ Age of Tyran = 9 + 9 = 18 years
Cost of tickets for adults = ₹ 6.00
Cost of tickets for children = ₹ 3.75
So, cost of tickets for Tyran's sisters
= 2 × 3.75 = ₹ 7.5
So, total money spent = ₹ 6.00 + ₹ 7.5 = ₹ 13.5

22. (a) Cost of tickets for parents = 2 × 6 = ₹ 12
So, total cost of tickets of all five members of family = ₹ 13.5 + ₹ 12 = ₹ 25.5
Total cost of snacks = ₹ 2.75 + ₹ 4.35 = ₹ 7.1
So, total money spent by the family
= ₹ 7.1 + ₹ 25.5 = ₹ 32.6

23. (a) Hourwise charges on Monday
10 am to 11 am = 1 × ₹ 1.50 = ₹ 1.50 (1 hour)
11 am to 5 pm = 6 × ₹ 2.20 = ₹ 13.2 (6 hours)
5 pm to 6 : 50 pm = 4 × ₹ 0.50 = ₹ 2
(approx 4 half hour)
Total charges on Monday
= ₹ (1.50 + 13.2 + 2) = ₹ 16.7

24. (b) Hourwise charges for Sunday
10 am to 11 am = 1 × ₹ 1.20 = ₹ 1.20 (1 hour)
11 am to 5 pm = 6 × ₹ 1.80 = ₹ 10.8 (6 hours)
5 pm to 6.50 pm = 4 × ₹ 2.20
= ₹ 8.8 (approx 4 half hour)
Total charges on Sunday = ₹ (1.20 + 10.8 + 8.8)
= ₹ 20.8
∴ Difference between the charges on Sunday and Monday = ₹ 20.8 − ₹ 16.7 = ₹ 4.1

Chapter 7 : Measurement

1. (b) Distance travelled by Ella starting from point A
= AB + BC + CD + DE + EF + FA
= 20 m + 20 m + 15 m + 9 m + 7 m + 10 m
= 81 m = 8100 cm [∵ 1 m = 100 cm]

2. (b) Distance between each plant
= 8 cm
Total length of boundary = 12 m
= 1200 cm [∵ 1 m = 100 cm]
So, number of plants which can be planted

$$= \frac{1200}{8} + 1 = 150 + 1 = 151$$

3. (c) Last year height of Jessy = 1 m 25 cm
Increase in height = 12 cm
So, present height of Jessy
= 1 m 25 cm + 12 cm = 1 m 37 cm
Height of Teresa = 1 m 8 cm
So, difference in the height of Jessy and Teresa = 1 m 37 cm − 1 m 8 cm = 29 cm

4. (c) Given, length of each saree = 8.28 m
Now, we will convert the metre in yards.
Now, 0.92 m = 1 yard

$$\therefore \quad 1 \text{ m} = \frac{1}{0.92} \text{ yard}$$

$$\Rightarrow \quad 8.28 \text{ m} = \frac{8.28}{0.92} \text{ yards}$$

$$= 9 \text{ yards}$$

So, measure of saree in yards is 9 yards.

5. (c) Length of shirt bought by Michelle
= 58.5 cm
∴ Required length of shirt
= 58.5 cm + 4 × 2.5 cm
= 58.5 cm + 10 cm = 68.5 cm
[∵ 1 inch = 2.5 cm]

6. (c) Weight of $\boxed{C}$ = 4 kg 800 g

$= 4000\text{ g} + 800\text{ g} = 4800\text{ g}$ [$\because$ 1 kg = 1000 g]

So, weight of $\boxed{A} = \frac{4800}{3} = 1600\text{ g}$ [$\because$ 1 C = 3A]

$\therefore$ Weight of $\boxed{B} = \frac{1600}{2} = 800\text{ g}$ [$\because$1 A = 2 B]

7. (b) Given, length of 1 small piece $= \frac{3}{5}$ m

$\therefore$ Length of 4 small pieces $= \frac{3}{5} \times 4 = \frac{12}{5}$

Also, given length of cloth left $= 4\frac{3}{5} = \frac{23}{5}$

$\therefore$ The total length of the cloth

$= \frac{12}{5} + \frac{23}{5} = \frac{35}{5} = 7\text{ m}$

8. (b) Given, 1 square = 5 circles

So, 2 squares = 10 circles

and 1 triangle = 4 circles

So, weight of 2 squares + 1 triangle + 1 circle

= (10 + 4 + 1) circles = 15 circles

Thus, 15 circles are required on the other side to balance the scale.

9. (d) Total weight of 2 pieces of gold

= 6 kg 755 g + 5 kg 550 g

= 6.775 kg + 5.550 kg [$\because$ 1 kg = 1000 g]

= 12.325 kg

Weight of biscuit to be made = 15 kg

So, weight of gold required = 15 kg − 12.325 kg

= 2.675 kg = 2 kg 675 g

10. (b)

I. True,

Total weight of candies = 3.6 kg + 0.75 kg

= 4.35 kg

Weight of each box $= \frac{4.35}{5}$ kg = 0.87 kg

II. False,

Vandy's height $= 1\frac{3}{8}\text{ m} = \frac{11}{8}\text{ m}$

Andy's height $= \frac{11}{8} + \frac{1}{4} = \frac{11+2}{8} = \frac{13}{8} = 1\frac{5}{8}$

III. False,

weight of each can $= \frac{13338}{9} = 1482\text{ L}$

IV. False, length of book is measured in metres or centimetre.

11. (b) Amount of water in the glass = 5 mL

Raise in height of water in glass after dropping the ball in it = 8 mL − 5 mL = 3 mL

Now, 1 mL = 1 cm^3

So, volume of one ball = 3 cm^3

$\therefore$ Total volume of all balls = Volume of five balls

$= 5 \times 3 = 15\text{ cm}^3$

12. (a) Volume of bath tub (in cubic m)

= 1.5 m × 0.7 m × 0.6 m = 0.63 cubic m

Now, 1 m^3 = 1000 L

So, 0.63 m^3 = 630 L

Now,

Volume of bath tub = Capacity of 10 buckets

i.e. Capacity of 10 buckets = 630 L

So, capacity of 1 bucket $= \frac{630}{10} = 63\text{ L}$

13. (c) Total quantity of water that need to be put

= 1 L

= 1000 mL [$\because$ 1 L = 1000 mL]

Capacity of container 1 = 150 mL

Capacity of container 2 = 25 mL

Now, we have

Option (a), 150 mL × 4 + 25 mL × 6 = 600 + 150

= 750 mL

Option (b), 150 mL × 8 + 25 mL × 3 = 1200 + 75

= 1275 mL

Option (c), 150 mL × 6 + 25 mL × 4 = 900 + 100

= 1000 mL

So, option (c) will be correct combination.

14. (b) Temperature shown in thermometer = 41° F

So, temperature (in °C) $= (41 - 32) \times \frac{5}{9}$

$\left[\because °C = (°F - 32) \times \frac{5}{9}\right]$

$= 9 \times \frac{5}{9} = 5°\text{ C}$

15. (c) Temperature at which the cake is to be baked

= 212° F

We know that, $°C = (°F - 32°) \times \frac{5}{9}$

So, we have $(212° - 32°) \times \frac{5}{9}$

$= 180° \times \frac{5}{9} = 100\text{ °C}$

16. *(a)*

I. $°F = 0° \times \frac{9}{5} + 32° = 32°\ F$

II. $°F = 100° \times \frac{9}{5} + 32° = 212°F$

III. $°F = 35° \times \frac{9}{5} + 32° = 63° + 32° = 95°\ F$

IV. Difference $= 35°C - 25°C = 10°C$

Now, $°F = 10° \times \frac{9}{5} + 32° = 18° + 32° = 50°F$

17. *(c)* Temperature of vessel I = 20° C

Temperature of vessel II = 35° C

So, difference of temperatures of vessels

$= 35°\ C - 20°\ C = 15°\ C$

Therefore, difference of temperature in fahrenheit

$= 15° \times \frac{9}{5} + 32° = 59°\ F \left[\text{as } °F = °C \times \frac{9}{5} + 32°\right]$

18. *(b)* From figure,

Total number of balls = 16

Total weight of balls = 360 gram.

$\therefore$ Weight of 1 ball $= \frac{360}{16} = 22.5$ gram.

Statement 1 Total weight of 12 balls

$= 22.5 \times 12 = 270$ gram

$= (30 \times 9)$ gram

$\therefore$ Value of weight of 12 such balls is 9th multiple of 30.

Statement 2 Weight of 8 balls

$= 22.5 \times 8 = 180$ gram.

and weight of 5 balls $= 22.5 \times 5 = 112.5$ gram.

$\therefore$ Their difference $= 180 - 112.5 = 67.5$ gram

$\therefore$ Weight of 8 such balls is 67.5 gram more than weight of 5 such balls.

$\therefore$ Statement-1 is true but Statement-2 is false.

19. *(a)* Volume of box 1 $= 30 \times 30 \times 12$ cubic ft

$= 10800$ cubic ft

Volume of box 2 $= 20 \times 20 \times 12$ cubic ft

$= 4800$ cubic ft

Volume of box 3 $= 10 \times 10 \times 12$ cubic ft

$= 1200$ cubic ft

So, total volume of three boxes

$= 10800 + 4800 + 1200$

$= 16800$ cubic ft

Number of small boxes = 140

$\therefore$ Volume of 1 small box

$= \frac{\text{Total volume of 3 boxes}}{\text{Number of small boxes}}$

$= \frac{16800}{140} = 120$ cubic ft

20. *(a)* From first watch, Kavya started studying at 4 : 25 O'clock.

According to the question, she studied 2 h 15 min first and again for another 1 h 45 min.

$\therefore$ Total time of study = 2 h 15 min + 1 h 45 min

= 4 h

from second watch, she stopped studying at 9 : 15 O'clock.

$\therefore$ Time period for her rest = 9 : 15 – (4:25 + 4) h

= 0 : 50 h

= 50 min

Chapter 8 : Shapes and Angles

1. *(a)* The angle formed by the arrow with the ground has measure greater than 90°, so it makes an obtuse angle with the ground.

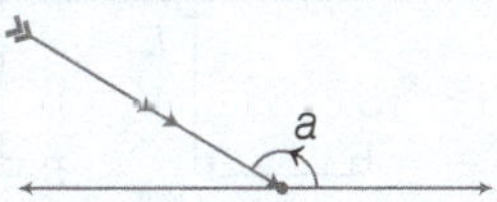

2. *(d)* The angle formed in figure (d) measures 90°, whereas the angles formed in other figures have measure greater than 90°, i.e. obtuse angles.

3. *(d)* Measure of angle in option (I) is less than 90°, so it is an acute angle.

Measure of angle in option (II) is equal to 90°, so it is a right angle.

Measure of angle in option (III) is greater than 90°, so it is an obtuse angle.

Measure of angle in option (IV) is greater than 180°, so it is an reflex angle.

Therefore, option (d) is correctly matched while others are not correctly matched.

4. *(c)* The measure of angles *a*, *b* and *d* is less than 90° but angle *c* is greater than 90°, so angle *c* is an obtuse angle.

5. *(b)*

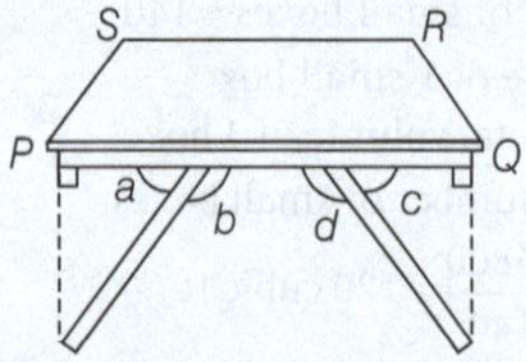

The foot of the left leg of the table makes an angle of 90°, when joined to *P*. So clearly $\angle a$ will be less than 90° i.e., acute and the another angle $\angle b$ will be more than 90° i.e., obtuse, similarly, $\angle c$ will be acute and $\angle d$ will be obtuse.

6. *(a)* The letters making acute angles are as follow :

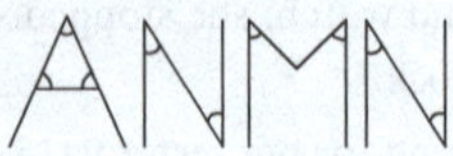

So, there are nine acute angles.

Hence, Neil is correct counting the number of acute angels.

7. *(c)*

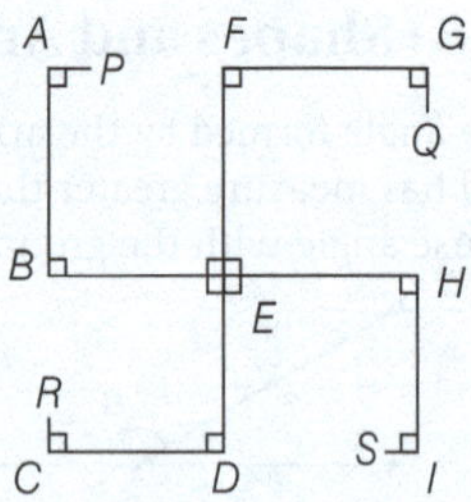

In the given figure, the number of right angles are $\angle BAP$, $\angle ABE$, $\angle BEF$, $\angle RCD$, $\angle CDE$, $\angle DEB$, $\angle QGF$, $\angle GFE$, $\angle FEH$, $\angle HIS$, $\angle IHE$, $\angle HED$

So, there are 12 right angles.

8. *(c)* It is clear from the figure that angle *a* and *b* are less than 90° and angle *c* and *d* are greater than 90°, so *c* and *b* are acute angles whereas *c* and *d* are obtuse. Also

$\angle DAE$, $\angle ADB$, $\angle BDC$, $\angle DCF$ are right angles. So only I and III are correct.

9. *(d)*

I. $\because$ Right angle = 90°

$\therefore \quad \frac{1}{2}$ right angle $= \frac{90°}{2} = 45°$

II. $\because$ Complete turn = 360°

$\therefore \quad \frac{3}{4}$ turn $= \frac{3}{4} \times 360° = 270°$

III. it will form a right (i.e. 90°) angle.

IV. $\angle ABC = \angle ABD + \angle DBE + \angle EBC$

$\Rightarrow 90° = 17° + \angle DBE + 32°$

$\Rightarrow \quad 90 = 49° + \angle DBE$

$\therefore \quad \angle DBE = 90° - 49° = 41°$

10. *(d)*

I. True, e.g. Rectangle  and square 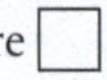

II. True, because 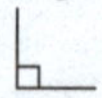

III. True, both have 90° angles

IV. False

$\because$ Complete turn = 360°

$\therefore \quad \frac{1}{4}$ turn $= \frac{360°}{4} = 90°$

11. *(b)*

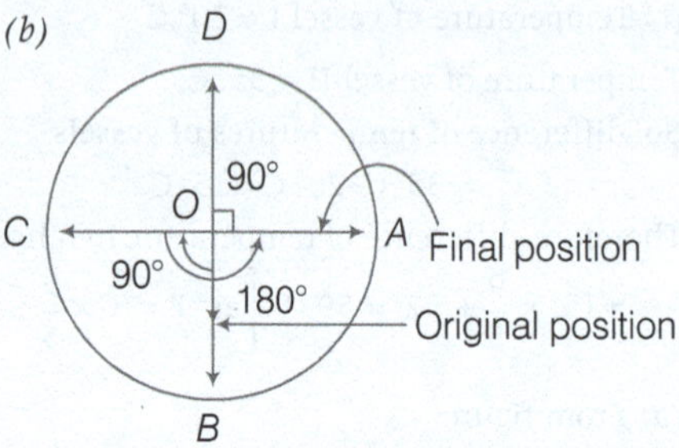

While turning 90° clockwise, the hour hand rests at *OC* and then turning 180° anti-clockwise, it rests at *OA*, hence $\angle DOA = 90°$

Thus, the angle formed by the minute and hour hands of the clock after rotation is 90°.

12. *(d)*

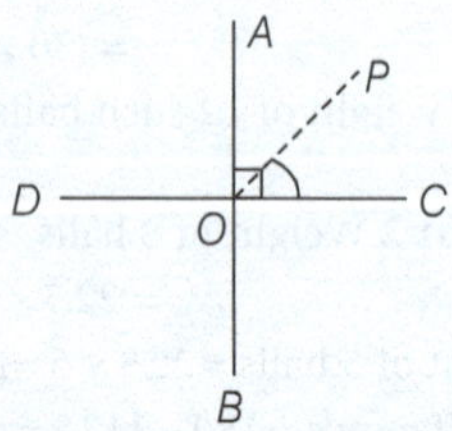

As it is clear from the figure OP bisects the right angle $\angle AOC$ (= 90°) in two equal halfs i.e. 45°, so each half of wing will make an angle of 45°.

13. *(b)* Only option (b) is open as its starting point and its end point do not coincide, whereas other figures are closed.

14. *(c)* Number of right angles formed in Fig. I = 0

[since, none of the angle is of 90° in the given figure]

Number of right angles formed in Fig. II = 2

Number of right angles formed in Fig. III = 1

So, on comparing, we get

II > III > I

15. *(c)* All shapes have equal number of sides but the angles formed are different. So, Kandy said the correct statement.

16. *(d)*

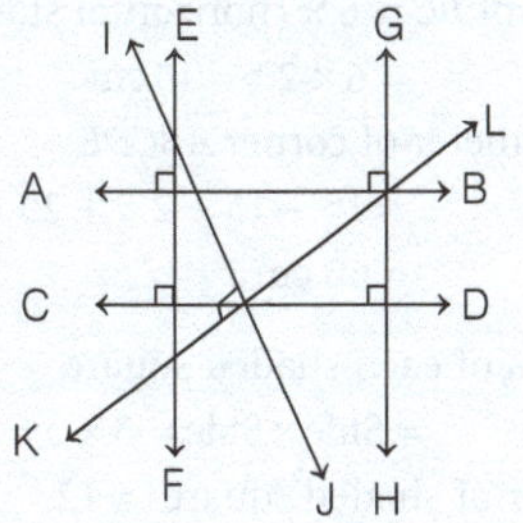

(i) There are 2 pair of parallel lines, which are AB and CD; EF and GH.

(ii) There are 5 pair of perpendicular lines as shown by in the given figure.

17. *(b)* On naming the given figure,

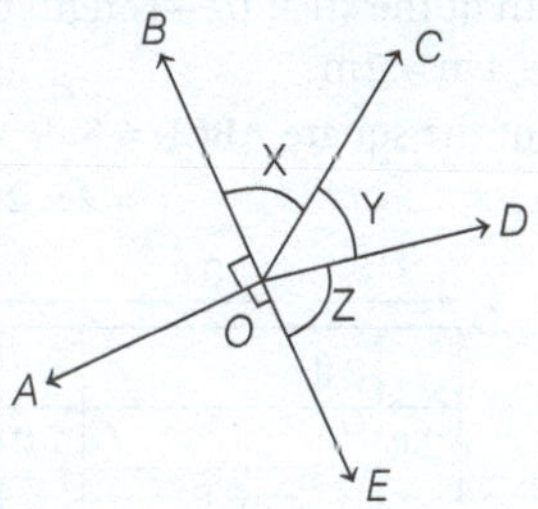

Here, BE is a straight line, so angle formed on either side of $BE = 180°$.

$\therefore \quad x + y + z = 180°$.

18. *(c)* **In slide I,**

$\angle B = 90°, \angle A = 20°, \angle C = a$

We have, $\angle A + \angle B + \angle C = 180°$

[since, sum of angles of a triangle = 180°]

$\angle C = 180° - \angle B - \angle A$

$\therefore \quad = 180° - 90° - 20°$

$\Rightarrow \quad \angle C = 90° - 20° = 70°$

In slide II,

$\angle B' = 90°, \angle A' = 35°, \angle C' = b$

We have, $\angle A' + \angle B' + \angle C' = 180°$

$\angle C' = 180° - \angle B' - \angle A'$

$= 180° - 90° - 35°$

$\Rightarrow \quad \angle C' = 90° - 35° = 55°$

Chapter 9 : Area and Perimeter

1. *(c)* Since, perimeter of a figure is the sum of the length of its sides. So, length of the border is an example of perimeter.

2. *(c)* The figure can be labelled as shown below

Perimeter of a figure

$= $ Sum of the length of its sides

$= AB + BC + CG + GF + FD + DE + EA$

$= AB + (BC + DE) + CG + GF + FD + EA$

But $\quad BC + DE = BE - CD = BE - GF$

$[\because CD = GF]$

$= 8\text{ cm} - 5\text{ cm} = 3\text{ cm}$

$\therefore$ Perimeter of figure $= 8 + 3 + 6 + 5 + 6 + 8$

$= 36\text{ cm}$

3. *(b)* Given, length of two sides (let) a and b are 75 m and 125 m respectively.

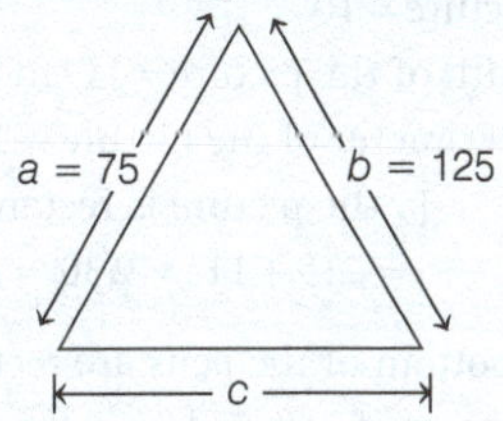

Let the third side of the triangle be c cm.

Given, perimeter of the triangle = 280 m.

We know, perimeter of a triangle = Sum of all its sides.

$\therefore \quad a + b + c = 280$

$\Rightarrow \quad 75 + 125 + c = 280$

$\Rightarrow \quad 200 + c = 280$

$\Rightarrow \quad c = 280 - 200 = 80\text{ cm}$

$\therefore$ The third side of the given triangle is 80 cm.

4. *(c)* Let the sides of a triangle be $2x$, $3x$ and $4x$ respectively.

According to the question,

We know that perimeter of triangle

$= $ sum of its all sides

$2x + 3x + 4x = 279$

$9x = 279 \Rightarrow x = \frac{279}{9} = 31$

$\therefore$ Length of each side $= 2x = 2 \times 31 = 62\text{m}$

$3x = 3 \times 31 = 93\text{m}$ and $4x = 4 \times 31 = 124\text{ m}$

5. (a) Perimeter of Fig. I = Sum of the lengths of sides

$= 5\text{ cm} + 2\text{ cm} + 2\text{ cm} + 2\text{ cm} + 2\text{ cm} + 2\text{ cm} + 5\text{ cm} + 2\text{ cm} + 2\text{ cm} + 2\text{ cm} + 2\text{ cm} + 2\text{ cm} = 30\text{ cm}$

Perimeter of Fig. II

= Sum of the lengths of sides

$= 1\text{ cm} + 3\text{ cm} + 2\text{ cm} + 2\text{ cm} + 2\text{ cm} + 1\text{ cm} + 1\text{ cm} + 3\text{ cm} + 6\text{ cm} + 3\text{ cm}$

$= 24\text{ cm}$

$\therefore$ Perimeter of Fig. I > Perimeter of Fig. II

So, Sanjay needs to colour the boundary for Fig. I more with a black pen.

6. (d) Number of marks made on length of the picture = 18

So, length of the picture = 19 cm

Similarly, number of marks made on the breadth of the picture = 10

$\therefore$ Breadth of the picture = 11 cm

Hence, perimeter of the picture $= 2(l + b)$

[$\because$ the picture is rectangular in shape]

$= 2(19 + 11) = 2(30) = 60\text{ cm}$

7. (a) The bottom of the pens are rectangle.

So, perimeter of Jolly's dogs pen $= 2(l + b)$

$= 2(8 + 12) = 2(20)$ [$\because l = 12\text{ cm}, b = 8\text{ cm}$]

$= 40\text{ cm}$

Now, perimeter of Ted's dogs pen $= 2(l + b)$

$= 2(6 + 15)$

$= 2(21) = 42\text{ cm}$

[$\because l = 15\text{ cm}, b = 6\text{ cm}$]

Therefore, Ted will use more fencing to make the pen.

8. (b) The stair corner is as follows :

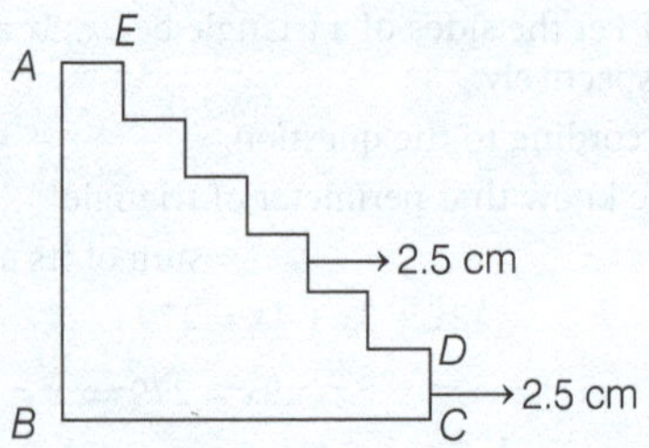

The perimeter of corner $ABCDE$

$= AB + BC + CD + DE + EA$

Since, height and width of each stair is 2.5 cm and 2.5 cm. Therefore length of one stair is 5 cm. In the given figure, there are five stairs.

So, distance from D to E is $5 \times 5 = 25\text{ cm}$.

Length $AB = 6 \times$ (vertical side of one stair)

$= 6 \times 2.5 = 15\text{ cm}$

Length of $BC = 6 \times$ (horizontal side of one stair)

$= 6 \times 2.5 = 15\text{ cm}$

$\therefore$ Perimeter of corner $ABCDE$

$= 15 + 15 + 2.5 + 25 + 2.5$

$= 60\text{ cm}$

9. (a) Area of each shaded square

$= \text{Side} \times \text{Side} = 3 \times 3 = 9\text{ cm}^2$

Number of shaded squares = 12

Area of all shaded squares

= Area of 1 shaded square

$\times$ Number of shaded squares

$= 9 \times 12 = 108\text{ cm}^2$

10. (b) Sides of the square $ABCD$

= Length of the stick ID – Length of stick DE

$= 6\text{ m} - 4\text{ m} = 2\text{ m}$

$\therefore$ Area of the square ABCD = Side $\times$ Side

$= 2 \times 2 = 4\text{ m}^2$

11. (b)

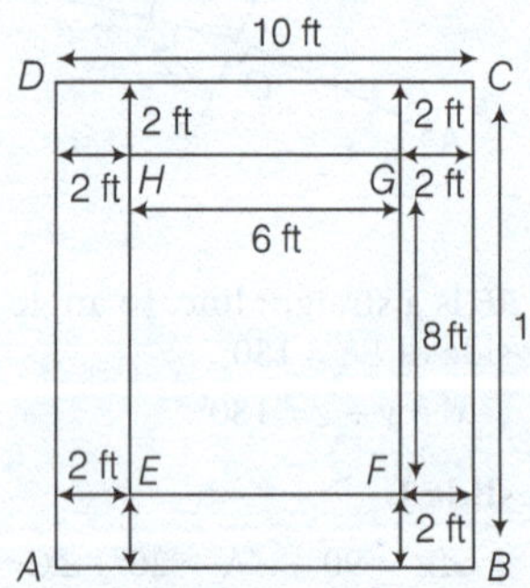

Length of the carpet = 12ft

Breadth of the carpet = 10ft

Area of the carpet $= l \times b = 12 \times 10 = 120$ sq ft

Area of rectangle $EFGH = 6\text{ ft} \times 8\text{ ft} = 48$ sq ft

$\therefore$ Area of border

= Area of carpet – Area of rectangle $EFGH$

$= 120 - 48 = 72$ sq ft

12. (c) We have,

$AG + AB + GF + BF = 8 + 8 + 8 + 8 = 32\text{ cm}$

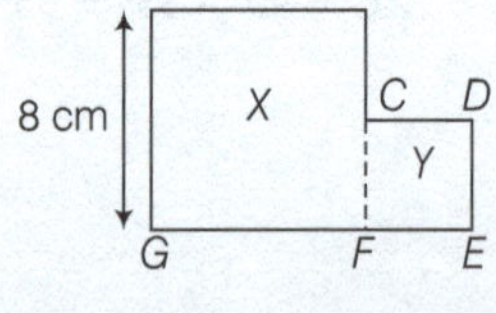

Now, the perimeter of figure is 40 cm.

$\therefore$ $32 + CD + EF = 40$

$\therefore$ $CD + FE = 40 - 32 = 8$ cm

and $CD = FE = 4$ cm [since, Y is a square]

Hence, area of $Y = 4 \times 4 = 16\text{ cm}^2$

13. *(c)* Perimeter of square I = 8 cm = $4 \times$ Side

Area of square II = 16 cm^2 = Side $\times$ Side

So, side of square II = 4 cm

$\therefore$ Perimeter of square II = $4 \times$ Side = $4 \times 4 = 16$ cm

So, the length of wire = Perimeter of square I + Perimeter of square II

= 8 cm + 16 cm = 24 cm

14. *(a)* Given, length of the rectangle (let) $l = 12$ cm

Let the breadth of the rectangle be b cm.

$\therefore$ Perimeter of rectangle = $2(l + b)$

$\therefore$ $2(l + b) = 36$ [$\because$ perimeter given]

$2(12 + b) = 36$

$\Rightarrow$ $12 + b = \frac{36}{2} = 18$

$b = 18 - 12 = 6$ cm

We know, area of the rectangle = $l \times b$

$\therefore$ Area $= 12 \times 6 = 72\text{ cm}^2$

15. *(d)* Area of rectangle = Length $\times$ Breadth = 42

$$\left.\begin{array}{l}\text{Option (a), Area of rectangle} = 1 \times 26 = 26\\ \text{Option (b), Area of rectangle} = 2 \times 13 = 26\\ \text{Option (c), Area of rectangle} = 2 \times 21 = 42\\ \text{Option (d), Area of rectangle} = 6 \times 7 = 42\end{array}\right\} \text{...(i)}$$

So, options (a) and (b) are eliminated, because area is not equal to 42 sq and

perimeter of rectangle = 26

$\Rightarrow$ $2(l + b) = 26$

So, $l + b = 13$

From Eq. (i), we have $6 + 7 = 13$

$\therefore$ $l = 6$ and $b = 7$

So, option (d) is correct.

16. *(a)*

I. True, 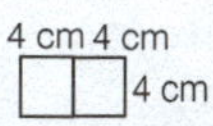

, so the length of rectangle formed = 8 cm

Breadth of rectangle formed = 4

$\therefore$ Perimeter = $2(l + b) = 2(8 + 4)$

$= 2 \times 12 = 24$ cm

II. False

e.g. Let length of rectangle = 3 and breadth = 2

So, area of rectangle = $3 \times 2 = 6$

Now, new length = 6

and new breadth = 4

$\therefore$ New area = $6 \times 4 = 24$, which is not doubled the original area.

III. True

Area of square = Area of rectangle

$= 8 \times 2\text{ cm}^2 = 16\text{ sq cm}^2$

$= 4 \times 4$

$\therefore$ Side of square = 4 cm

17. *(b)* For maximum area of rectangle, we consider length = 26 m, breadth = 24 m

$\therefore$ Maximum area for rectangle = 26×24

$= 624\text{ m}^2$

For maximum area of square, we consider a side 25 cm.

Maximum area of a square

$= 25 \times 25 = 625\text{ m}^2$

Maximum area for $\frac{1}{2}$ rectangle + $\frac{1}{2}$ square

$= \frac{624}{2} + \frac{625}{2} = \frac{1249}{2}$

$= 624.5\text{ m}^2$

Hence, square will have the maximum area.

18. *(c)* We have,

(a) Perimeter = $2(20 + 20) = 2(40) = 80$ m

(b) Perimeter = $2(40 + 10) = 2(50) = 100$ m

(c) Perimeter = $2(4000 + 0.1) = 2(4000.1)$

$= 8000.2$ m

So, he must choose the land having boundary given in option (c).

19. *(a)* Area of classroom

$= l \times b = 18 \times 22$ sq ft = 396 sq ft

Space occupied by a bench = $l \times b$

$= 4 \times 2.5$ sq ft = 10 sq ft

Space occupied by 28 such benches

$= 10 \times 28 = 280$ sq ft

Space occupied by almirah = $l \times b = 5 \times 4$ sq ft

= 20 sq ft

Space occupied by table = $l \times b = 3 \times 5$ sq ft

= 15 sq ft

So, space left = Area of classroom
– (Area of 28 benches + Almirah + table)
= 396 – (280 + 20 + 15) = 81 sq ft

20. (*c*) Total breadth of class III A, V and II
= Length of assembly ground = 6 m

So, breadth of each class = 2 m [∵ 6 ÷ 3 = 2]
and length of each class = 4 m

∴ Area of a class $= l \times b = 4 \times 2 = 8\ \text{m}^2$

So, area covered by 12 such classes $= 12 \times 8 = 96\ \text{m}^2$

21. (*a*) Area of assembly ground
$= l \times b = 6 \times 3 = 18\ \text{m}^2$

So, area of hall $= \frac{2}{3} \times 18 = 12\ \text{m}^2$

Now, length of hall = Length of three classes
= 6 m

So, breadth of hall = Area ÷ Length
= 12 ÷ 6 = 2 m

∴ Perimeter of hall $= 2(l + b) = 2(6 + 2)$
$= 16\ \text{m}^2$

Chapter 10 : Pattern and Symmetry

1. (*b*) As the ball is being rotated 180° clockwise, then in the next figure the ball will look like

2. (*b*) Figure (b) is the correct the other half of the given figure.

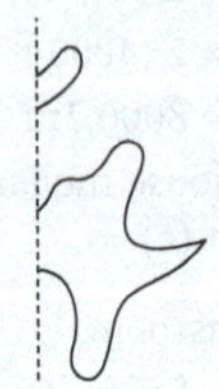

3. (*d*) The given series of picture follows the pattern similar as
A A B C A A A B B C A A A A B B B C C
So, option (d) is correct.

4. (*c*) The number pattern is as follows :

$7 + 7 \to 7 + 7 - 2 = 12$
$4 + 4 \to 4 + 4 - 2 = 6$
$3 + 3 \to 3 + 3 - 2 = 4$
$2 + 2 \to 2 + 2 - 2 = 2$
So, $8 + 8 \to 8 + 8 - 2 = 14$

5. (*c*) The pattern is that a square is added in each step first at right side, then at top, then at left side and then at bottom.

So, the shape term will be

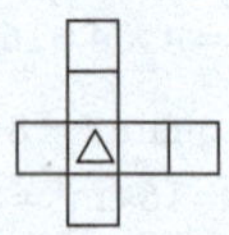

6. (*c*) Given pattern of numbers is as follows :

$1 = 0 \times 9 + 1$

$11 = 1 \times 9 + 2$

$111 = 12 \times 9 + 3$

So, we have

1111 → Four 1's $= 123 \times 9 + 4$

7. (*d*) The series of books is as follows :

3, 6, 12, ...
×2 ×2

So, we have 1st, 2nd, 3rd, 4th, 5th, 6th, 7th, 8th and so on as follows :

3, 6, 12, 24, 48, 96, 192, 384, ...

So, number of books on fifth rack is 48.

8. (*d*) The series of items put in the boxes is as follows :

I	II	III	IV	V	VI	VII	VIII	IX	X
58,	69,	80,	91,	102,	113,	124,	135,	146,	157

+11 +11 +11 +11 +11 +11 +11 +11 +11

So, 157 items will be put in the 10th box.

9. (*d*) The given figure has 5 lines of symmetry passing through each of the vertex *A*, *B*, *C*, *D* and *E* as shown below :

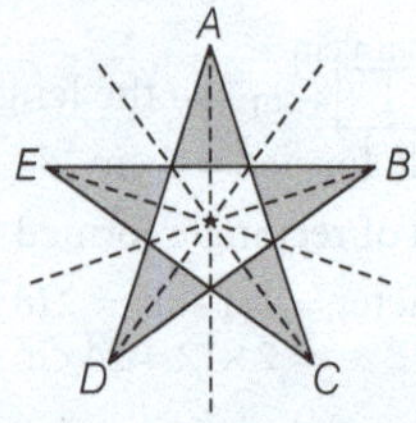

10. (*b*) The lines of symmetry of each letter of the word are given below :

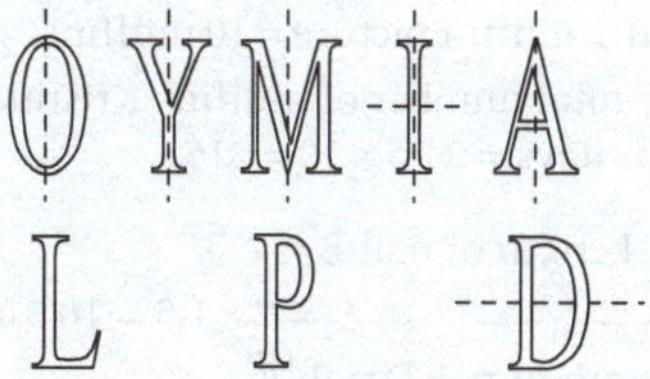

So, 5 letters have a vertical line of symmetry.

11. (*d*) On rotating half a turn the figures will become as follows

Figure (d) will look same on turning half a turn as it has rotational symmetry.

12. (*c*) The given figure has followswing line of symmetry :

I. 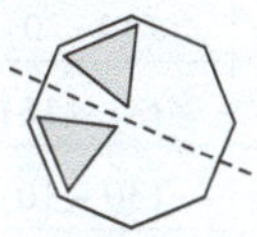 II. 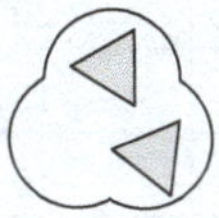 No line of symmetry

III.  IV.  No line of symmetry

Only Fig. III has vertical line of symmetry.

13. (*d*) None of the letters given in option is symmetrical as pattern of given figure.

14. (*c*) The figure of the given cards half turned is as follows

So, only card I looks the same after taking half turn.

15. (*b*)

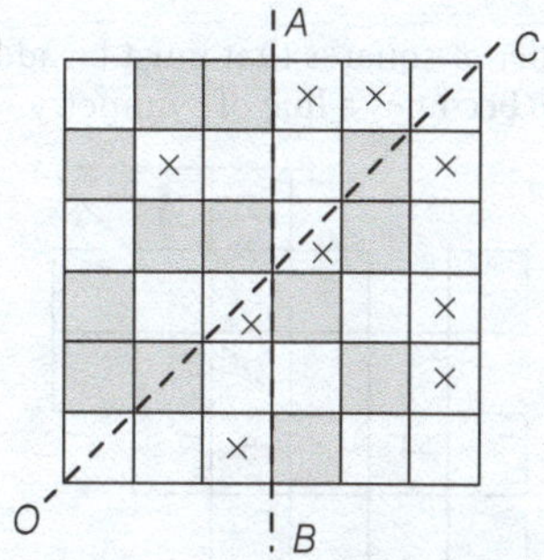

The number of squares having a cross sign should be shaded to make the given figure symmetrical about the line *AB*, which is obtained by folding the given figure along the line *AB*.

∴ Number of squares with cross sign = 9

16. (*b*) The number series of the toffees is as follows

1 coin → 5 ; 2 coins → 5 + 3 → 8

3 coins → 8 + 3 → 11 ; 4 coins → 11 + 3 → 14

5 coins → 14 + 3 → 17

6 coins → 17 + 3 → 20

So, 7 coins → 20 + 3 → 23.

Hence, sherry get 23 toffees.

17. (*a*) Here, the series of figures depends on the last column of each figure which contains the following number of triangles :

I	II	III	IV
2	3	4	5

So, the total number of triangles used in the last and second last column of 17th pattern is

18 + 17 = 35

18. (*c*) We have the series as follows :

$1 + 2 + 3 + 4 + 5 + 6 + 7 + 8 + 9 + 10 = 55$

$11 + 12 + 13 + 14 + 15 + 16 + 17 + 18 + 19 + 20 = 155$

$41 + 42 + 43 + 44 + 45 + 46 + 47 + 48 + 49 + 50 = 455$

So, $91 + 92 + 93 + 94 + 95 + 96 + 97 + 98 + 99 + 100 = 955$

$\therefore$ $91 + 92 + 93 + 94 + 95 + 96 + 97 + 98 + 99 = 955 - 100$

19. (*c*) 8 number of squares that must be added so that the line *AB* becomes a line of symmetry.

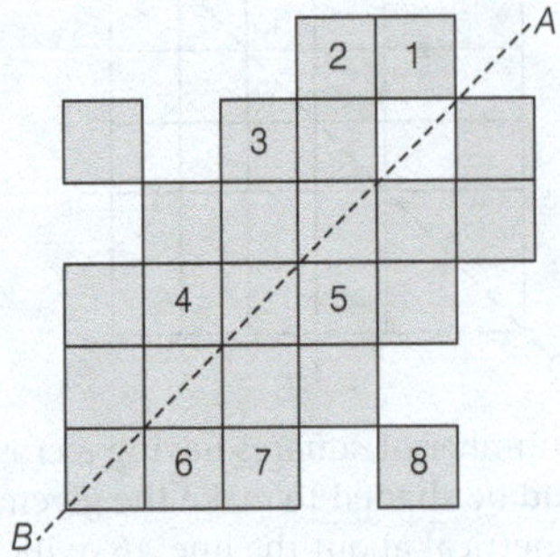

20. (*d*)

(i) False. There is one line of symmetry in

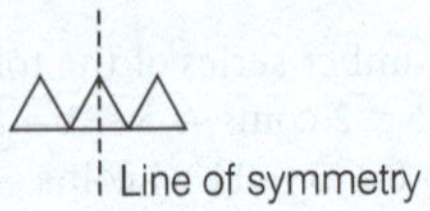

(ii) True. There are two lines of symmetry in

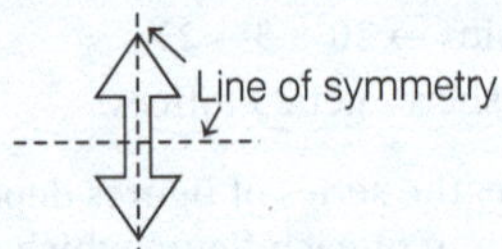

(iii) True. A circle has infinite lines of symmetry.

Chapter 11 : Data Handling

1. (*c*) Given,  = 10, then 45 = 40 + 5

= 10 + 10 + 10 + 10 + 5

= 

2. (*d*) Number of orders completed in week 2

= 10 + 10 + 10 + 5 = 35 [∵ □ = 10, ▯ = 5]

So, number of orders completed in week 3

= 35 − 15 = 20

= □□

3. (*a*) Total number of figures made = 25

and total number of students = 50

So,

 = $\frac{\text{Total number of students}}{\text{Total number of figures made}} = \frac{50}{25}$ = 2 students

4. (*c*) Total number of muffins in the picture = 21.5

and 1 muffin picture = 10 muffins

So, total number of muffins Kristine baked in four days = 21.5 × 10 = 215

5. (*c*) Length of nail B = 7 ⊤

= 7 × 1.5 = 10.5 units

Length of nail D = 9 ⊤

= 9 × 1.5 = 13.5 units

∴ Required difference = 13.5 − 10.5 = 3 units

Solutions (Q. Nos. 6-8)

6. (*d*) The following table shows the number of sunny days and rainy days.

Months	Sunny days	Rainy days
January	14	(31 − 14) = 17
February	6	(28 − 6) = 22
March	16	(31 − 16) = 15
April	20	(30 − 20) = 10
May	18	(31 − 18) = 13
June	10	(30 − 10) = 20

So, month June had 20 rainy days.

7. (*c*) Number of sunny days during the first three months = 14 + 6 + 16 = 36

8. (*c*) Month having highest number of rainy days = February (22).

9. (*b*)

I. ↓ = 5

↓↓↓↓↓ = 5 × 5 = 25

II.  = 70

 = $\frac{70}{2}$ = 35

III. 12 ☆ = 72

So, 1 ☆ = $\frac{72}{12}$ = 6

IV. ◇◇ = 24,

So, ◇ = $\frac{24}{2}$ = 12

$\therefore$ 11 ◇ $= 11 \times 12 = 132$

Now, $132 = 11$◇

10. (a) We have by tally marks 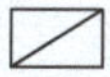 = 5

Tally marks representing super market

= 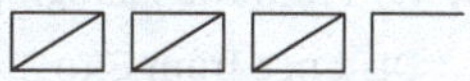

$\therefore$ Number of people who went to super market

$= 5 + 5 + 5 + 2 = 17$

11. (b) Number of people who went to post office

= 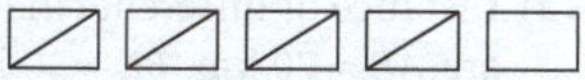

$= 5 + 5 + 5 + 5 + 4 = 24$

Number of people who went to shoe shop

= 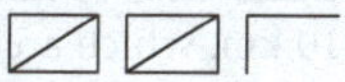

$= 5 + 5 + 2 = 12$

$\therefore$ Required difference $= 24 - 12 = 12$

12. (a) The taxi driver made the most journeys on Tuesday (36).

So, total money collected on Tuesday

$= 36 \times 112 =$ ₹4032

13. (c) Number of journeys made on Monday = 23

Money collected on Monday

$= 23 \times 85 =$ ₹ 1955

Number of journeys made on Wednesday = 18

Money collected on Wednesday $= 18 \times 69$

= ₹1242

$\therefore$ Required difference = ₹1955 − ₹1242

= ₹ 713

14. (b) From the graph we can make the following table

Literature	Number of students in class V(A)	Number of students in class V(B)
Fantasy	9	4
Folk tales	6	6
Science fiction	8	12
Sports	9	9

Thus, fantasy literature is more preferred in class V (A) than in class V (B).

The difference between the number of students who preferred fantasy in class V (A) than in class V (B) $= 9 - 4 = 5$

15. (c) Number of birthdays in each month.

Months	Number of birthdays	Months	Number of birthdays
January	2	November	0
February	1	December	2
March	6		
April	1		
May	7		
June	1		
July	3		
August	1		
September	2		
October	1		

So, only two months have number of birthdays more than 4 namely March (6) and May (7).

16. (c) Number of children having birthdays coming after 31st January and before 1st July = Number of children having birthdays between 1st February and 30th June $= 1 + 6 + 1 + 7 + 1 = 16$

17. (b) Maximum number of books read (by Javed) = 15

and minimum number of book read (by Tom) = 5

$\therefore$ Required difference $= 15 - 5 = 10$ books

18. (b) Capacity of tank when completely filled with water = 120 L

So, capacity of tank when half-filled with water

= 60 L

$\therefore$ Time taken for the tank to be half-emptied

$= 2{:}30 - 1 = 1.5$ h

19. (d) The number of hours each child watch the TV is given below :

Mary → 21
Peter → 15
David → 9
John → 15
Susan → 14
Mark → 11
Clarie → 22
Jane → 12
Paul → 18

So, Susan watched TV 14 h a week.

20. (c) Total of three maximum number of hours $= 22 + 21 + 18$

= 61 h (from above question)

Total of three minimum number of hours the children have watched TV = 9 + 11 + 12

= 32h

∴ Required difference = 61 − 32h = 29 h

Solutions (Q.Nos. 21-24) Given, total number of vehicles = 7000

21. *(a)* Lorries ratio from the pie chart = $\frac{3}{25}$ of total number of vehicles = $\frac{3}{25} \times 7000 = 840$

22. *(c)* Ratio of others vehicles from pie chart

$$= 1 - \left(\frac{1}{4} + \frac{19}{50} + \frac{3}{25} + \frac{9}{50}\right)$$

$$= 1 - \left(\frac{25 + 38 + 12 + 18}{100}\right)$$

$$= 1 - \frac{93}{100} = \frac{7}{100}$$

According to the question, 30% of others are cycles.

∴ Number of cycles = $30\% \times \frac{7}{100} \times 7000$

$$= \frac{30}{100} \times \frac{7}{100} \times 7000 = 147$$

23. *(b)* From the pie chart,

Ratio of Trucks = $\frac{9}{50}$

and ratio of lorries = $\frac{3}{25}$

∴ Ratio of number of trucks to that of lorries

$$= \frac{\frac{9}{50}}{\frac{3}{25}} = \frac{9}{50} \times \frac{25}{3}$$

$$= \frac{3}{2} = 3:2$$

24. *(a)* From the pie chart,

Ratio of cars = $\frac{19}{50}$ of total vehicles,

Ratio of motor cycles = $\frac{1}{4}$ of total vehicles.

∴ Number of More cars than motor cycles

$= \left(\frac{19}{50} - \frac{1}{4}\right)$ of total vehicles

$= \left(\frac{38 - 25}{100}\right)$ of total vehicles

$= \frac{13}{100}$ of total vehicles

$$= \frac{13}{100} \times 7000 = 910$$

25. *(c)* From the pictograph

Distance from E to A = 50 km

E to B = 40 km

E to C = 20 km

E to D = 60 km

(a) Distance of different cities from E are AE = 70 km, BE = 30 km, CE = 90 km, DE = 60 km, which are not correct.

(b) AE = 50 km, BE = 40 km, CE = 60 km, DE = 110 km, which are not correct.

(c) AE = 50 km, BE = 40 km, CE = 20 km, DE = 60 km, which are correct.

(d) AE = 90 km, BE = 60 km, CE = 20 km, DE = 40 km, which are not correct.

26. *(c)* Picture used to number of books read in August = $11\frac{1}{2}$ 📖

If 1 📖 = 2 books,

so $11\frac{1}{2}$ 📖 = 11.5 📖 = 11.5 × 2

= 23 books

∴ Number of books read in August = 23

27. *(c)*

If 1 📖 = 4 books, then books read in June

= 10 × 2

= 20 = 5 × 4

(📖📖📖📖📖)

= 5 📖

[because, now 📖 means 4 books]

28. *(d)* Temperature on Wednesday = 27.5° C

Temperature on Saturday = 15° C

∴ Difference = 27.5° C − 15° C = 12.5° C

29. *(a)* Temperature on each day is as follows

Sunday	→	125° *C*
Monday	→	17.5° *C*
Tuesday	→	225° *C*
Wednesday	→	27.5° *C*
Thursday	→	15° *C*
Friday	→	17.5° C
Saturday	→	15° *C*

Hence, on Tuesday the temperature was near $22.5°C$ which is between $27°C$ and $18°C$.

30. *(c)* Percentage of students choose apple as their favourite fruit = 25%

$\therefore$ Number of students choose chickoo

$= \frac{10}{25} \times 15 = 6$

31. *(d)* Part of orange is more in pie chart, so orange is the most popular fruit.

Percentage of students who like orange

= 30%

Here, grapes percentage

$= 100 - (25 + 30 + 15 + 20) = 10\%$

Least popular fruit is grapes with percentage

= 10%

$\therefore$ Required ratio $= \frac{30}{10} = 3:1$

Practice Set 1

1. *(d)* Angle C is an obtuse angle as its measure is greater than 90°.

2. *(b)* The pattern is as follows :

$(14 + 7) \div 3 = 7$

$(17 + 8) \div 5 = 5$

So, $(22 + 6) \div 7 = 4$

3. *(d)* Number of cubes in top row = 5

Number of cubes in middle row = 5 + 3 = 8

Number of cubes in last row = 8 + 4 = 12

So, total number of cubes = 5 + 8 + 12 = 25

4. *(c)*

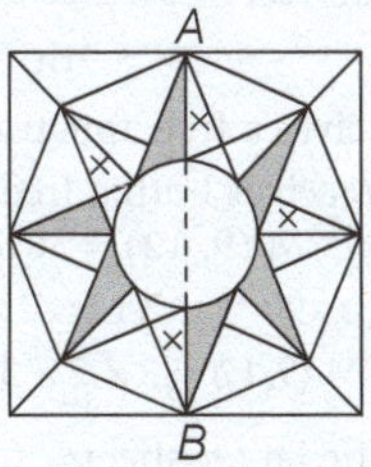

The places in the figure, which are crossed, are required to be shaded to make AB as its line of symmetry.

So, the number of triangles to be shaded to make AB as the line of symmetry is 4.

5. *(b)* Total number of pupils = 50 + 120 + 90 + 20

= 280

Number of pupils who go by car = 90

So, the required fraction $= \frac{90}{280} = \frac{9}{28}$

6. *(c)* We have, $x + 2 \times 6 \div 3 = 52$

$\therefore \quad x + 2 \times \frac{6}{3} = 52$

$\Rightarrow \quad x + 2 \times 2 = 52$

$\Rightarrow \quad x + 4 = 52$

$\therefore \quad x = 52 - 4 = 48$

7. *(d)* Only the net of cube in option (d) will have no two faces having same alphabet meeting to form an edge.

8. *(b)* Quantity of flour in bag A = 15 kg

After pouring some quantity of flour in bag B from bag A, quantity of flour in bag B = 8 kg

So, remaining quantity of flour in bag A

= 8 + 3 = 11 kg

$\therefore$ Quantity of weight transferred from bag A to bag B = 15 − 11 = 4 kg

9. *(d)* Length of 1 blue ribbon = 204 cm

Length of 5 blue ribbons = 204 × 5 = 1020 cm

Total length of blue and yellow ribbons

= 22.84 m = 2284 cm [$\because$ 1 m = 100 cm]

$\therefore$ Length of 8 yellow ribbons = 2284 − 1020

= 1264 cm

So, length of 1 yellow ribbon = 1264 ÷ 8 = 158 cm

10. *(c)* Difference between average maximum and average minimum temperature of different cities are as follow :

New Delhi = 38°C − 32°C = 6°C

Kolkata = 39°C − 27°C = 12°C

Chennai = 40°C − 28°C = 12°C

Mumbai = 32°C − 28°C = 4°C

So, Mumbai had the least difference between its average maximum and average minimum temperature.

11. *(a)* Length of 1 brick = 0.2 m = 20 cm

[$\because$ 1 cm = 100 cm]

Breadth of 1 brick = 0.08 m = 8 cm

Height of 1 brick = 6 cm

So, volume of 1 brick $= l \times b \times h$

$= 20 \times 8 \times 6 = 960 \text{ cm}^3$

Now, length of wall = 10 m = 1000 cm

Breadth of wall = 0.06 m = 6 cm

Height of wall = 200 cm

So, volume of wall $= 1000 \times 6 \times 200$

$= 1200000 \text{ cm}^3$

$\therefore$ Number of bricks $= \dfrac{1200000}{960} = 1250$

12. (*b*) Greatest number of students that could be arranged in each row = HCF (144, 128)

$= 2 \times 2 \times 2 \times 2 = 16$

13. (*b*) Length of track I = 8 m

and breadth of track I = 6 m

So, perimeter of track I $= 2(l + b) = 2(8 + 6)$

$= 2(14) = 28$ m

Length of track III $= (8 + 3 + 3 + 2 + 2)$ m

$= (8 + 6 + 4)$ m $= 18$ m

and breadth of track III

$= 6 \text{ m} + 3 \text{ m} + 3 \text{ m} + 2 \text{ m} + 2 \text{ m}$

$= 6 \text{ m} + 6 \text{ m} + 4 \text{ m} = 16 \text{ m}$

So, perimeter of track III $= 2(18 + 16)$

$= 2(34) = 68$ m

$\therefore$ Difference of perimeters $= 68 \text{ m} - 28 \text{ m}$

$= 40$ m

14. (*c*)

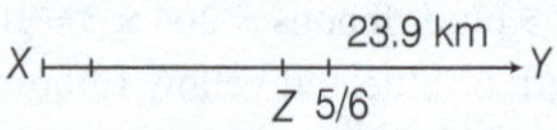

Fraction of journey completed $= \dfrac{5}{6}$

Fraction of journey left $= 1 - \dfrac{5}{6} = \dfrac{1}{6}$

So, total distance $= 23.9 \text{ km} \times 6$

$= 143.4$ km

Therefore, the distance between town *X* and town $Z = \dfrac{1}{2}(143.4) = 71.7$ km

15. (*d*) Amount of money Jack had

$= \dfrac{2}{5}$ amount of money Kerry had

Amount of money Jack had $+ 12.40 = \dfrac{3}{4}$

(amount of money Kerry had $-$ 12.40)

So, $\dfrac{2}{5}$ amount of money Kerry had $+ 12.40$

$= \dfrac{3}{4}$ amount of money Kerry had $- 9.3$

$\Rightarrow \dfrac{3}{4}$ amount of Kerry had $- \dfrac{2}{5}$ amount of money Kerry had $= 12.40 + 9.3$

$\Rightarrow \dfrac{7}{20}$ of money Kerry had $= 21.7$

So, money Kerry had $= \dfrac{21.7 \times 20}{7} =$ ₹ 62

16. (*d*) We have,

__ 1 (units digit) [from Step I]

↑

$2 \times (2 \div 2) - 1 = 2 \times 1 - 1 = 2 - 1 = 1$

[from Step II]

3 (tens digit) 1

↑

15 subtracted from 36 and then divided by 7

$= (36 - 15) \div 7 = 21 \div 7 = 3$ [from Step III]

So, the number is 31.

17. (*c*) I. We know from divisibility test, a number is divisible by 9, if the sum of the digits of the number is divisible by 9.

e.g. In number 243,

Sum of digits $= 2 + 4 + 3 = 9$ and $243 \div 9 = 27$

II. XI + XVI + XX $= 11 + 16 + 20 = 47$

III. 100×20

IV. units, tens and hundred

18. (*c*) Multiple of

6 = 6, 12, 18, 24, 30, 36, 42, 48, 54, 60

These all are even numbers. They have 6, 2, 8, 4, 0 as the unit digit.

Since, 6, 18, 30,... are not divisible by 12.

These all are divisible by 3.

So, Chrish is correct.

19. (*c*) Visit in which Saran receives a free beverage

= 9th

Visit in which she receives a free appetiser = 12th

Visit in which Saran receives both a free beverage and a free appetiser = LCM (9, 12) = 36th

[as $9 = 3 \times 3, 12 = 2 \times 2 \times 3$, so

LCM $(9, 12) = 2 \times 2 \times 3 \times 3 = 36$]

20. (*d*) The perimeter of the larger sheet

= LCM (3, 4, 5) $= 3 \times 2 \times 2 \times 5 = 60$ units

As,

3	3, 4, 5
2	1, 4, 5
2	1, 2, 5
5	1, 1, 5
	1, 1, 1

21. (*d*) I. True, 1 is a factor of even number.
II. True, 0 is neither a prime number nor a composite number.
III. False, LCM of two number × HCF of two numbers = Product of two numbers
IV. False, HCF of two coprime numbers = 1

22. (*a*) Total money saved by the six friends

$= ₹\,210 + ₹\,300 + ₹\,50 + ₹\,100 + ₹\,95 + ₹\,245$

$= ₹\,1000$

Now, $\frac{1}{20}$th part of the whole amount $= \frac{1}{20} \times 1000$

$= ₹\,50$

Here, Kim saved $₹\,50 = \frac{1}{20}$th part of the whole amount.

Hence, option (a) is correct.

23. (*c*) We have,

$$\frac{7}{9} \times \frac{4}{4} = \frac{28}{36} \text{ or } \frac{28}{36} \div \frac{4}{4} = \frac{7}{9}$$

Similarly,

$$\frac{12}{20} = \frac{3}{5} \times \frac{4}{4}$$

and $\frac{16}{28} = \frac{4}{7} \times \frac{4}{4}$

So, group *A* is obtained by multiplying the numerator and denominator of group *B* by 4.

24. (*b*) We have, 3 cups = 1 jar

So, $\frac{1}{2}$ jar $= \frac{3}{2}$ cups

To pour the juice that fills the jar half full, number of cups required $= \frac{3}{2}$ cups

Now, cups of orange juice poured

$= \frac{1}{2}$ cup

So, total number of cups of juice poured

$= \frac{3}{2} + \frac{1}{2} = \frac{4}{2} = 2$ cups

Now, amount of jar filled by 3 cups = 1

So, amount of jar filled by 1 cup $= \frac{1}{3}$

Therefore, amount of jar filled by 2 cups

$= \frac{2}{3}$ or two-third.

25. (*b*) The correct ascending order of the sugar bags according to their weight is

$$6.08 < 6.10 < 6.18 < 6.80 < 6.81$$

26. (*b*) Emma's mass = 4.65 kg

and Zua's mass = 5.25 kg

∴ Difference between their masses

$= (5.25 - 4.65)$ kg

$= 0.60$ kg or 600 g [∵ 1 kg = 1000 g]

27. (*d*) Joy's mass = 3.75 kg

and Luca's mass = 4.96 kg

∴ Total mass = (3.75 + 4.96) kg = 8.71 kg

28. (*c*) Here, 1 toy block = 1 cube of volume 1 cubic unit

∴ Number of toy blocks = Volume of the stack

$= 3 \times 4 \times 3 = 36$

29. (*b*) Volume of box 1 = 2 cm × 3 cm × 4 cm

= 24 cubic cm

Volume of box 2 = 3.5 cm × 1.5 cm × 0.05 m

= 3.5 cm × 1.5 cm × 5 cm

[∵ 1 m = 100 cm]

= 26.25 cubic cm

So, volume of box 2 > volume of box 1.

Therefore, the height of water of vessel in which box 2 is dipped will raise more.

30. (*d*) $\angle B = 90°$ [given]

Sum of the angles of a triangle = 180°

i.e. $\angle A + \angle B + \angle C = 180°$

So, the sum of the measure of other two angles,

i.e. $\angle A + \angle C = 180° - 90° = 90°$

31. (*b*) The measure of angles formed in a polygon is

$P \rightarrow$ less than 90° $\rightarrow$ Acute angle

$Q \rightarrow$ equal to 90° $\rightarrow$ Right angle

$R \rightarrow$ greater than 90° $\rightarrow$ Obtuse angle

$S \rightarrow$ greater than 90° $\rightarrow$ Obtuse angle

$T \rightarrow$ equal to 180° $\rightarrow$ Straight angle

32. (a)

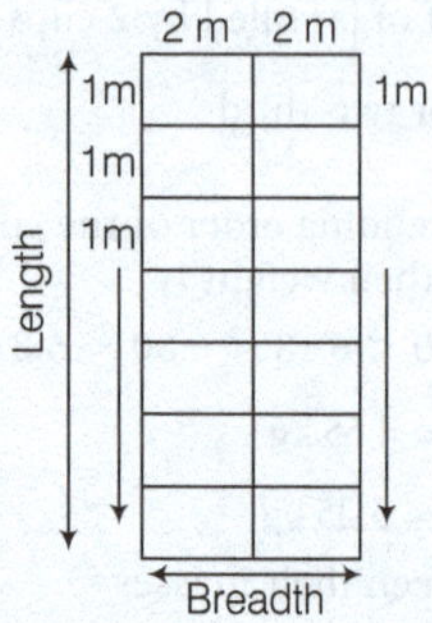

Given, the breadth of the space where one car is parked = 2 m

The length of the space where one car is parked

= 1 m

So, the length of the rectangular parking lot

$= 1 \times 7 = 7$ m

[where, 7 is the number of rows of car spaces]

and breadth $= 2 \times 2 = 4$ m

[where, 2 is the number of columns of car spaces]

$\therefore$ Area of the parking lot $= 4 \times 7 = 28$ sq m

33. (b) Length of the court = 50 ft

Breadth of the court = 30 ft

$\therefore$ Area of the court $= l \times b = 50 \times 30$

$= 1500$ sq ft

Paint required to cover 150 sq ft = 2 L

$\therefore$ Paint required to cover 1500 sq ft

$= \frac{2}{150} \times 1500 = 20$ L

[by using unitary method]

34. (a) We have, figure as follows :

A → non-symmetrical → ✓

B → symmetrical → ✗

C → symmetrical → ✗

D → non-symmetrical → ✓

35. (a) Fig. (i) is folded, it will form a cube with square faces.

Fig. (ii) is folded, it will form square pyramid.
Fig. (iii) is folded, it will form cuboid with rectangular faces and when Fig. (iv) is folded, it will form a prism.

I. → (i) ; II. → (ii) ; III. → (iv); IV. → (iii)

36. (c) Number 17675 when rounded off to nearest thousands gives 18000.

37. (a) 9th multiple of 19 is $= 9 \times 19 = 171$

7th multiple of 17 is $= 7 \times 17 = 119$

$\therefore$ Required quantity $= 171 - 119 = 52$

38. (d) Julee birthday party starts at = 11 : 20 am

Party finished 3 h 30 min later.

$\therefore$ Party finished at time = 11 : 20 am + 3 h 30 min

= 2 : 50 pm

39. (c) Sum of 4 angles of a quadrilateral = 360°

Here, sum of 3 angles of a quadrilateral = 290°

$\therefore$ 4th angle of the quadrilateral = 360° − 290° = 70°

40. (b) There are four right angles outside in the given figure.

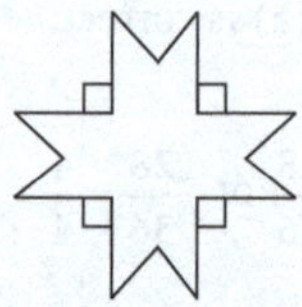

41. (c) We have the following operations :

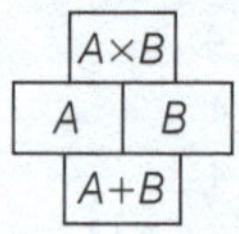

So, we have

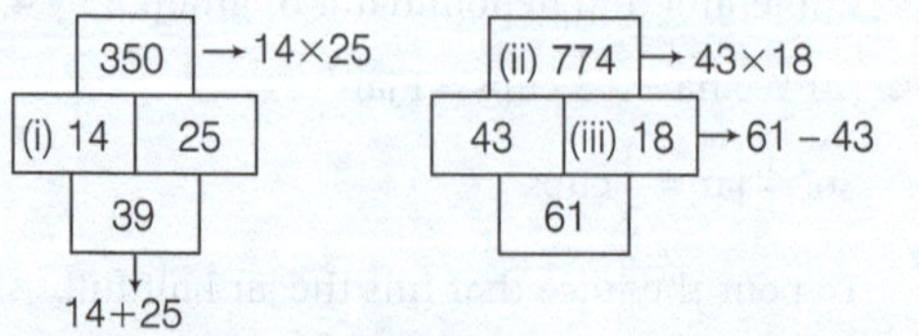

(i) → 14, (ii) → 774, (iii) → 18

42. (b) Total cost of a pair of jeans, a black shirt and a brown bag from shop 1

= ₹ 1147.21 + ₹ 534.23 + ₹ 520.12

= ₹ 2201.56

Total cost of a pair of jeans, a black shirt and a brown bag from shop 2

= ₹ 1272.46 + ₹ 324.49 + ₹ 420.41 = ₹ 2017.36

Total cost of a pair of jeans, a black shirt and a brown bag from shop 3

= ₹ 1014.76 + ₹ 576.23 + ₹ 500.29

= ₹ 2091.28

Arranging the cost in descending order, we get
2201.56 > 2091.28 > 2017.36
The total cost is least from shop 2, so she should buy the items from shop 2.

43. (*a*) Quantity of lemon juice in 1 bottle

$= 1100 \text{ mL}$

Quantity of lemon juice in 2 such bottles

$= 1100 \text{ mL} \times 2$

$= 2200 \text{ mL}$

Now, amount of water in which 220 mL of lemon juice is mixed = 770 mL
So, amount of water in which 2200 mL of lemon juice is mixed $= \left[\dfrac{770}{220} \times 2200\right]$

$= 7700 \text{ mL}$

$\therefore$ Total amount of lemonade made

$= 2200 + 7700 \text{ mL}$

$= 9900 \text{ mL}$

$= 9000 \text{ mL} + 900 \text{ mL}$

$= 9 \text{ L } 900 \text{ mL}$ $\quad [\because 1 \text{ L} = 1000 \text{ ml}]$

44. (*b*) In clock I, the angle made between the hands

$= 180° - 35° - 55°$

$[\because$ sum of all three angles of a triangle is $180°]$

$= 180° - 90° = 90°$

In clock II, the angle between the hands

$= 180° - (75° + 40°)$

$= 180° - 115° = 65°$

In clock III, the angle made between the hands

$= 180° - (35° + 20°)$

$= 180° - 55° = 125°$

In clock IV, the angle made between the hands

$= 180° - (45° + 25°)$

$= 180° - 70° = 110°$

45. (*a*) Given, a wall

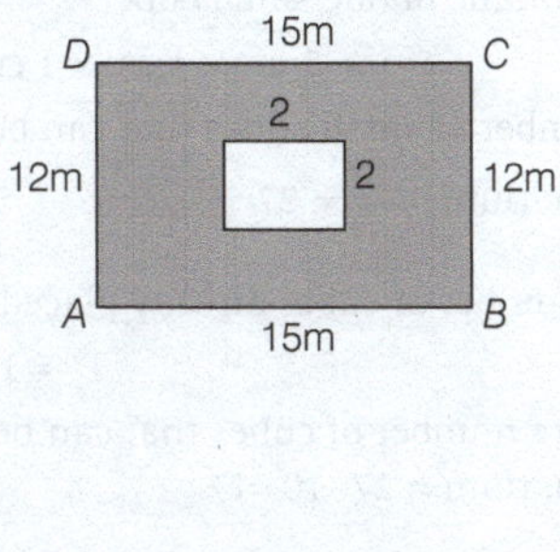

Before knowing the cost of painting, we would need to know the area of the wall (shape as a rectangle).
Area of the region to be painted

= Area of wall − Area of window

$\therefore$ Area of the wall = length × breadth

$= 15 \times 12 = 180 \text{ m}^2$

Area of window = side × side $= 4 \text{m}^2$

Area of painted region $= 180 - 4 = 176 \text{ m}^2$

$\because$ Cost of painting = ₹ 50/100 m^2

$\therefore$ Total cost of painting

$= \dfrac{50}{100} \times 176 =$ ₹88

46. (*c*) According to the given pattern, we have

Figure	Number of triangles	Number of square
I	4 ← 1 × 2 + 2	1
II	6 ← 2 × 2 + 2	2
III	8 ← 3 × 2 + 2	3
IV	10 ← 4 × 2 + 2	4

So, the number of triangles in the 11th picture of the given pattern $= 11 \times 2 + 2 = 24$

47. (*c*) Only two digits '0' and '3' have atleast one line of symmetry.

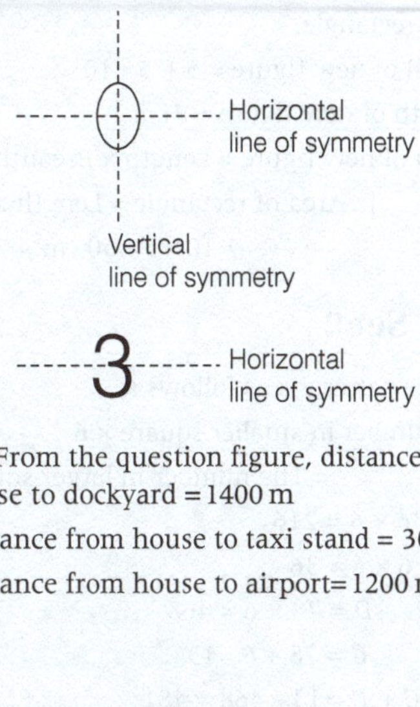

48. (*a*) From the question figure, distance from house to dockyard = 1400 m
Distance from house to taxi stand = 300 m.
Distance from house to airport= 1200 m.

Distance from house to bus stop = 900 m
and distance to railway station = 900 m.

$\therefore$ Option (a) shows the correct Bar graph.

49. *(b)* Total number of students in a class = 160

$\therefore$ Number of boys in class $= \frac{3}{8}$ of 160

$$= \frac{3}{8} \times 160 = 60$$

Number of boys which wear bracelet

$$= \frac{1}{3} \text{ of } 60$$

$$= \frac{1}{3} \times 60 = 20$$

Number of girls in class $= 160 - 60 = 100$

Number of girls which wear bracelet

$$= \frac{4}{5} \text{ of } 100 = \frac{4}{5} \times 100 = 80$$

$\therefore$ Total number of students which wear bracelet

$$= 20 + 80 = 100$$

50. *(a)* Side of square boxes = 5 cm

Renu get a new figure, joint two square boxes

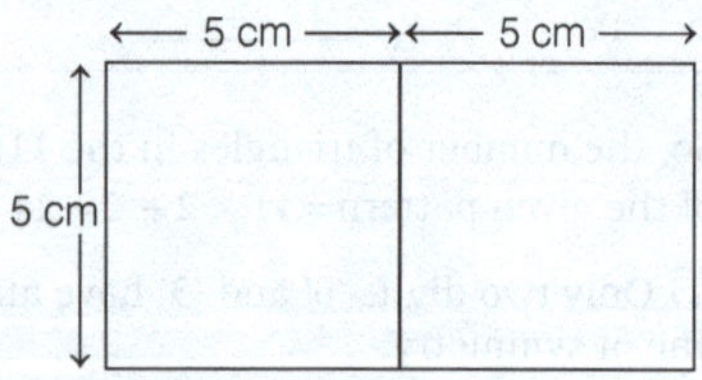

It is a rectangle.

Length of new figure $= 5 + 5 = 10$

Breadth of new figure = 5 cm

$\therefore$ Area of new figure = Length × Breadth

[$\therefore$ Area of rectangle = Length × Breadth]

$$= 10 \times 5 = 50 \text{ cm}^2$$

Practice Set 2

1. *(b)* The pattern is as follows :

The number in smaller square × 6

= The number in larger square

i.e. $36 \times 6 = 216$

$6 \times 6 = 36$

So, $D = 78 \times 6 = 468$

and $C = 78 \div 6 = 13$

$\therefore$ $C + D = 13 + 468 = 481$

2. *(c)* We have, $P = 4595$

So, $71099 - 4595 = 66504 = 67000$

[rounding off to nearest thousand]

3. *(c)* Distance covered in one time = 2.5 mile

So, total distance covered $= 3 \times 25$ mile

$= 7.5$ mile

Hence, option (c) is correct.

4. *(c)* The length of bigger rectangle = 14 cm

Breadth of bigger rectangle = 6 cm

$\therefore$ Area of bigger rectangle $= 14 \times 6 = 84 \text{ cm}^2$

Length of smaller rectangle $= 14 - (8 + 2)$

$= 4$ cm

Breadth of smaller rectangle $= 6 - 4 = 2$ cm

$\therefore$ Area of smaller rectangle $= 4 \times 2 = 8 \text{ cm}^2$

$\therefore$ Area of shaded part $= 84 - 8 = 76 \text{ cm}^2$

5. *(b)* Let,  = A,  = B

and  = C

Then, $A - B = 50 \Rightarrow B = A - 50$ ...(i)

$C - A = 20 \Rightarrow C = A + 20$ ...(ii)

and $B + A + C = 240$

$\Rightarrow A - 50 + A + A + 20 = 240$

$\Rightarrow 3A = 340 - 20 + 50 \Rightarrow 3A = 270$

$\Rightarrow A = 70$

$\therefore$ $C = 70 + 20$

or  = 90

6. *(c)* Volume of aquarium = 3 cm × 3 cm × 3 cm

$= 27 \text{ cm}^3$

Now, volume of one small cube

$= 1 \text{ cm} \times 1 \text{ cm} \times 1 \text{ cm} = 1 \text{ cm}^3$

So, number of small cubes that can be placed in the aquarium $= \frac{27}{1} = 27$

Now, number of cubes already placed

$= 1 + 3 + 6 = 10$

So, more number of cubes that can be placed in the aquarium $= 27 - 10 = 17$

7. (*c*) According to the pattern,

19 = 

8. (*b*) The shortest height at which the two stacks of boxes will be of the same height

= LCM of the heights of boxes

= LCM (12, 18) = 36 inch

$[\because 12 = 2 \times 2 \times 3 \text{ and } 18 = 2 \times 3 \times 3]$

9. (*c*) Distance between Andy's and Sam's house rounding to nearest hundred = 4400 m

Distance between their houses rounding to nearest thousand = 4000 m

$\therefore$ Required difference = 4400 m − 4000 m

= 400 m

10. (*c*) Given, $1 + 1 = 11 = (1 \times 1)\ (1 \times 1)$

$2 + 2 = 44 = (2 \times 2)\ (2 \times 2)$

$3 + 4 = 916 = (3 \times 3)\ (4 \times 4)$

So, $4 + 5 = (4 \times 4)\ (5 \times 5) = 1625$

11. (*d*)

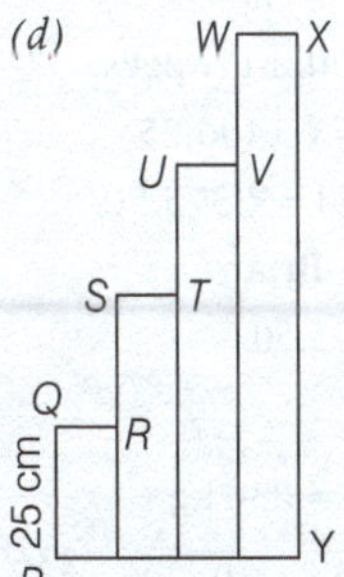

Fig. (A)

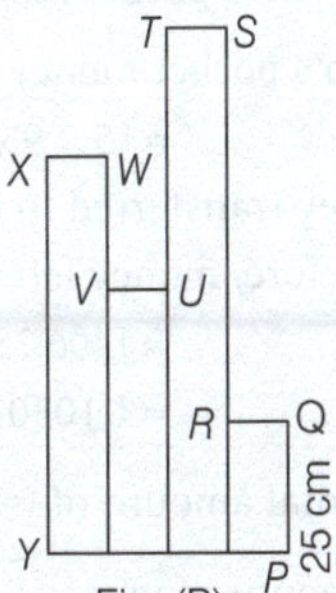

Fig. (B)

Perimeter of figure *A*

$= PQ + QR + RS + ST + TU + UV + VW + WX + XY$

= 25 cm + 10 cm + 25 cm + 10cm + 25 cm + 10 cm + 25 cm + 10 cm + 100 cm = 240 cm

Perimeter of figure *B*

$= PQ + QR + RS + ST + TU + UV + VW + WX + XY$

= 25 cm + 10 cm + 75 cm + 10 cm + 50 cm + 10 cm + 25 cm + 10 cm + 75 cm

= 290 cm

So, difference in perimeters

= 290 cm − 240 cm

= 50 cm

12. (*b*) 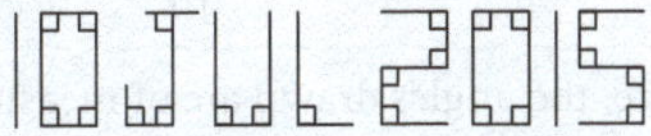

Number of right angles in letters = 6

Number of right angles in numbers = 16

$\therefore$ Required difference = 16 − 6 = 10

13. (*d*)

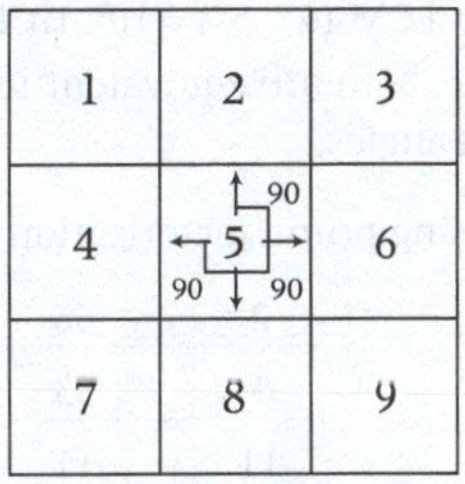

$90° + 90° + 90° = 270°$

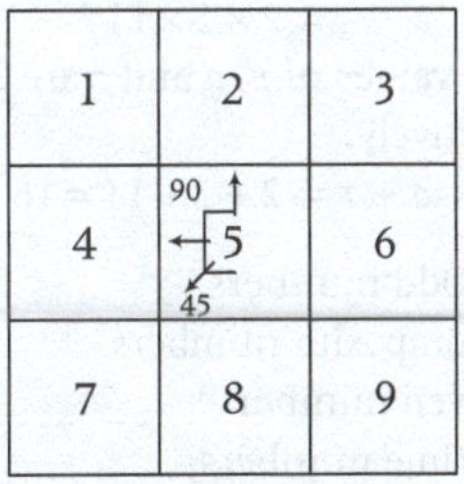

$90° + 45° = 135°$

Shimpy would have faced box 7, if turned 135° to the left.

14. (*b*) Rainfall in July, 14 = 6.2 cm

Rainfall in August, 13 = 1.8 cm

So, difference = 6.2 − 1.8 cm = 4.4 cm

15. (*a*) Money used first = $\frac{4}{9}$ of total money

Money left = $\left(1 - \frac{4}{9}\right)$ of total money

= $\frac{5}{9}$ of total money

Fraction of money used again $= \frac{1}{3} \times \frac{5}{9} = \frac{5}{27}$

Fraction of money left $= \frac{5}{9} - \frac{5}{27} = \frac{10}{27}$

Amount left = ₹ 330

So, we have $\frac{10}{27}$ of total money = ₹ 330

So, first of total money $= \frac{330 \times 27}{10}$ = ₹ 891

16. (*c*) Here, the angles drawn are of measure 50°, 80 °, 110°, 140°.

Now, HCF (50°, 80°, 110°, 140°) = 10°

[as $50 = 5 \times 5 \times 2$, $80 = 2 \times 2 \times 2 \times 2 \times 5$, $110 = 2 \times 5 \times 11$, $140 = 2 \times 2 \times 5 \times 7$]

Now, LCM (2°, 5°) = 10°, HCF (10°, 100°) = 10°

Hence, both are equivalent to relation of the given angles.

17. (*c*) Using prime factorisation method,

2	66
3	33
11	11
	1

$= 2 \times 3 \times 11$

∴ The values of p, q and r are 2, 3 and 11 respectively.

∴ $p + q + r = 2 + 3 + 11 = 16$

18. (*d*) I. Odd numbers

II. Composite numbers

III. Even numbers

IV. Prime numbers

19. (*b*) Jessica's square shows the fraction $= \frac{2}{8} = \frac{1}{4}$

and Denmark's square shows the fraction $= \frac{4}{8} = \frac{1}{2}$

Now, option (b) represents $\frac{2}{5}$.

On comparing $\frac{2}{5}, \frac{1}{2}$ and $\frac{1}{4}$ by converting them into equivalent fractions, we get

$$\frac{8}{20}, \frac{10}{20}, \frac{5}{20}$$

So, $$\frac{5}{20} < \frac{8}{20} < \frac{10}{20}$$

∴ $$\frac{2}{5} < \frac{1}{2} \text{ but } \frac{2}{5} > \frac{1}{4}$$

Hence, option (b) will be Andrew's square.

20. (*c*) Total number of hours worked in a week = 15

Number of hours worked on Monday $= 3\frac{1}{2} = \frac{7}{2}$

Number of hours worked on Tuesday = 4

Number of hours worked on Wednesday

$= 2\frac{1}{6} = \frac{13}{6}$

Number of hours worked on Thursday $= 1\frac{1}{2} = \frac{3}{2}$

So, total number of hours worked in four days

$= \frac{7}{2} + 4 + \frac{13}{6} + \frac{3}{2} = \frac{21 + 24 + 13 + 9}{6} = \frac{67}{6}$

So, number of hours worked on Friday

= Total number of hours worked in a week – Total number of hours worked in four days

$= 15 - \frac{67}{6} = \frac{90 - 67}{6} = \frac{23}{6} = 3\frac{5}{6}$ h

21. (*d*) Brian's pocket money = 15 pounds

Brian's pocket money in Indian rupees

$= 15 \times 93.75$ = ₹ 1406.25

Money transferred to friend = ₹ 375.50

Therefore, money left with Brian

$= 1406.25 - 375.50$

= ₹ 1030.75

22. (*d*) Total amount of wheat = 236 kg

∴ Amount of wheat 1 person will get $= \frac{236}{16}$

On dividing, 16)236(14.75

```
16↓
 76
 64
 120
 112
  80
  80
   ×
```

So, each one will get 14.75 kg of wheat.

23. *(b)* Given, Time = 4 h

Distance = 95 km

We know that, Speed $= \frac{\text{Distance}}{\text{Time}}$

$\therefore$ Speed of the cyclist $= \frac{95}{4}$ km/h

Now, to convert this fraction into its decimal equivalent number we will divide.

```
4)95(23.75
  8
  --
  15
  12
  --
   30
   28
   --
    20
    20
    --
     ×
```

$\therefore$ Speed = 23.75 km/h.

24. *(b)* Capacity of the locker

= Length × Breadth × Height

= 12 inch × 8 inch × 30 inch

= 2880 cubic inch

Volume of 1 book = 24 cubic inch

So, number of books which can be placed in the locker $= \frac{\text{Capacity of locker}}{\text{Volume of book}} = \frac{2880}{24} = 120$

25. *(d)* Volume of cuboid shaped gold biscuits

$= 30\text{ cm} \times 20\text{ cm} \times 0.05\text{ m}$

$= 30\text{ cm} \times 20\text{ cm} \times 5\text{ cm}$ [$\because$ 1 m = 100 cm]

$= 3000\text{ cm}^3$

Volume of cube shaped brick

$= 1.2 \times 1.2 \times 1.2\text{ m}^3$

$= 1.728\text{ m}^3 = 1728000\text{ cm}^3$

So, number of gold biscuits which can be formed

$= \frac{\text{Volume of cube shaped brick}}{\text{Volume of cuboid shaped biscuits}}$

$= \frac{1728000}{3000} = 576$

26. *(b)*

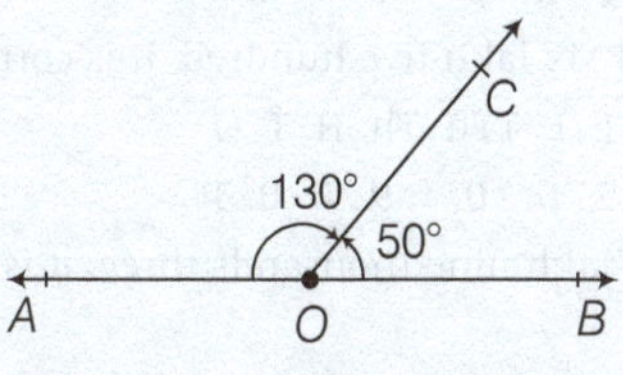

By using protractor we see that, with base *OB*, the angle formed is of measure 50°, but with base *OA* the same angle is of measure 130°.

27. *(d)* Area of square sheet of poster board

$= (l \times b) = 12 \times 12 = 144$ sq inch

Area of one invitation card $= l \times b = 2 \times 3$

= 6 sq inch

So, the number of cards that can be made

$= \frac{\text{Area of square sheet}}{\text{Area of card}}$

$= \frac{144}{6} = 24$

28. *(d)* Size of a page of scrap book = 7.5 by 6 cm

Area of the page of the scrap book $= l \times b$

$= 7.5 \times 6$

$= 45\text{ cm}^2$

Area of each stamp $= l \times b = 2.5 \times 1.5$

$= 3.75\text{ cm}^2$

So, number of stamps in one page

$= \frac{\text{Area of page of the scrap book}}{\text{Area of one stamp}}$

$= \frac{45}{3.75} = 12$

$\therefore$ Number of stamps in 10 such pages

$= 12 \times 10 = 120$

29. *(c)* Joining the pieces of option (c) to make the given cube.

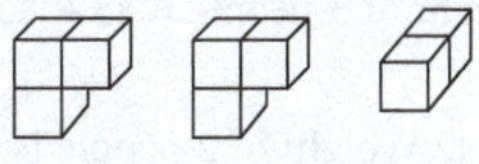

we get 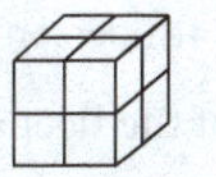

30. *(a)* Product of 9787 and 6879 =

```
     9787
   × 6879
   ------
    88083
   68509×
  78296××
 58722×××
 --------
 67324773
```

Required number =

$$\begin{array}{r} 67324773 \\ -\ 7556456 \\ \hline 59768317 \end{array}$$

31. (c) The set of all the prime number between 1 to 30 = {2, 3, 5, 7, 11, 13, 17, 19, 23, 29}

32. (c) According to the question,

$$\frac{3}{5} - X = \frac{7}{15}$$

$$\Rightarrow \quad X = \frac{3}{5} - \frac{7}{15} = \frac{9-7}{15} = \frac{2}{15}$$

33. (c) Expanded form of the decimal 70.0302

$$= 70 + \frac{0}{10} + \frac{3}{100} + \frac{0}{1000} + \frac{2}{10000}$$

$$= 70 + \frac{3}{100} + \frac{2}{1000}$$

34. (b) The largest 7 digit number = 9999999

∴ The value of successor of the largest 7 digit number = 9999999 + 1 = 10000000

35. (d) Jaspreet joined cooking classes on 18th march 2019.

Jaspreet completed cooking classes on 30th June 2019.

∴ The duration of the classes

$= (14 + 30 + 31 + 30)$ days $= 105$ days

36. (b) Total weight of 4 people = 406 kg

Total weight of 3 people = 83 + 83 + 79

= 245 kg

[∴ Weight of 2 people is equal i.e. 83 kg]

∴ Weight of 4th person = 406 − 245 = 161 kg

37. (c) Length of the floor = 25 m

Let the breadth of the floor be x m,

∴ Perimeter of floor $= 2(l + b)$

$$\Rightarrow \quad 74 = 2(25 + x)$$

$$\Rightarrow \quad 37 = 25 + x$$

$$\Rightarrow \quad x = 37 - 25 = 12\text{m}$$

∴ Area of floor $= l \times b = 25 \times 12 = 300\text{m}^2$

38. (a) Radius of the circle $r = 6.3$ cm

∴ Circumference of the circle $= 2\pi r$

$$= 2 \times \frac{22}{7} \times 6.3$$

$$= 2 \times 22 \times 0.9 = 39.6 \text{ cm}$$

39. (a) Total stitches = 848

Number of stitches in a row = 32

$$\begin{array}{r} 32)848(26 \\ 64 \\ \hline 208 \\ 192 \\ \hline 16 \end{array}$$

∴ The number of complete rows = 26

40. (d) The number of students who participated in school B = 480

The number of students who participated in school D and G = 440 + 400 = 840

∴ Required number of students = 840 − 480

= 360

41. (d) Given, opening time of showroom on Wednesday = 9 : 30 am.

and Sameer arrived at the showroom at 8 : 15 am.

∴ Waiting time on Wednesday = 9 : 30 − 8 : 15

= 1 : 15 = 1 h 15 min

Now, opening time of showroom on Sunday

= 9 : 45 am

and Sameer arrived at showroom at 8 : 15 am.

∴ Waiting time on Sunday = 9 : 45 − 8 : 15

= 1 : 30 = 1 h 30 min

42. (b) XX = 10 + 10 = 20, LIV = 50 + 4 = 54

LXVI = 50 + 10 + 6 = 66, LIX = 50 + 9 = 59

XCVII = (100 − 10) + 7 = 97

and LXXXVIII = 50 + 30 + 8 = 88

∵ 20 < 54 < 59 < 66 < 88 < 97

∴ XX < LIV < LIX < LXVI < LXXXVIII < XCVII

43. (b)

(a)

TL	L	TTh	Th	H	T	O
4	6	0	0	5	0	0

i.e. forty six lakh five hundred, it is correct.

(b)

TL	L	TTh	Th	H	T	O
5	0	0	9	0	0	3

i.e Fifty lakh nine thousands three, it is not correct.

(c) Number 82464 is rounded off to nearest tens is 82460, which is in correct.

(d) Predecessor of 999999 is 999998, which is correct.

44. *(d)* We have,

□ × □ = 36

As 6 × 6 = 36, so □ = 6

Also, ○ ÷ □ = 8 or 48 ÷ 6 = 8

So, ○ = 48

and ✡ + ○ = 50 ⇒ ✡ = 50 − 48 = 2

∴ □ + ○ + ✡ = 6 + 48 + 2 = 56

45. *(c)* Sum of place values of 6 = 6000 + 60 + 0.6

= 6060.6

Sum of place values of 3 = 3 + 0.03 = 3.03

∴ Required difference = 6060.6 − 3.03

= 6057.57

46. *(c)* Let Kishan's monthly salary be ₹ x.

According to the question,

$$\frac{x}{3} + 1700 = x$$

$$\Rightarrow \quad x - \frac{x}{3} = 1700$$

$$\Rightarrow \quad \frac{3x - x}{3} = 1700$$

$$\Rightarrow \quad \frac{2x}{3} = 1700$$

$$\Rightarrow \quad x = 1700 \times \frac{3}{2}$$

∴ Kishan earn in a year $= 1700 \times \frac{3}{2} \times 12$

= ₹ 30600

47. *(a)* From figure,

∠AOR is an acute angle.

∠POR is a right angle, it is not an obtuse angle.

∠AOQ is an obtuse angle, it is not a straight angle

.

∠DOB is a right angle, it is not an acute angle. Hence, option (a) is correct answer.

48. *(b)* The given figure divided the following parts

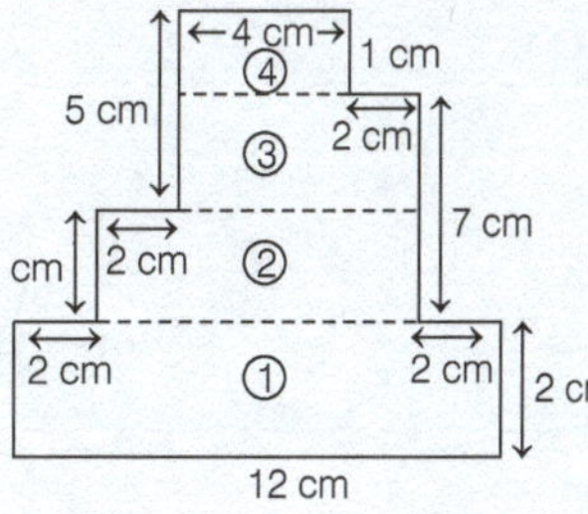

Area of given figure = Area of fig 1 + Area of fig 2 + Area of fig 3 + Area of fig 4

= (12 × 2) + (8 × 3) + (6 × 4) + (4 × 1)

[∵ figure gives 1, 2, 3 and 4 are rectangle and Area of rectangle = Length × Breadth]

= 24 + 24 + 24 + 4 = 76 cm²

49. *(d)*

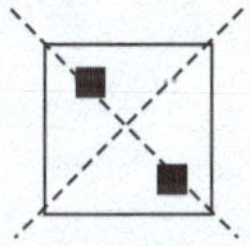

There are 2 symmetrical lines.
i.e. (p) → (z)

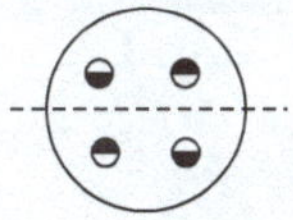

There is 1 symmetrical line.
i.e. (q) → (y)

There is 1 symmetrical line.
i.e. (r) → (y)

So, option (d) is correct answer.

50. *(c)* Number of visitors of place C = 18000

∴ Number of visitors of place

E = 18000 + 5000 = 23000

∴ Total number of visitors

= Number of visitors of place A, B, C, D and E

= 20000 + 15000 + 18000 + 30000 + 23000

= 106000